THE HOUR
BEFORE THE DAWN

by

GODFREY WINN

COLLINS

48 PALL MALL LONDON

1942

NOTE

All the royalties from this book are being given
to the King George Fund for Sailors.

Much of the material here is included by kind
permission of the Editor of the *Sunday Express*,
and many of the photographs are the work
of Ivor Castle. The frontispiece appears by
courtesy of Fox Photos Ltd.

I also wish to acknowledge with gratitude the
generous gesture of Lieut. Peter Scott in allow-
ing me to reproduce on the cover of this book a
photograph of a picture painted by him, another
photographic replica of which is to be found
facing page 56.

To

JOHN GORDON

MY EDITOR, CRITIC AND FRIEND,

this book is gratefully dedicated.

PROLOGUE

IN an hour, I am off to catch yet another train to yet another unknown destination. My bag is packed, my desk is cleared. Outside the night is quiet except for the persistent rain which makes me wonder uneasily, what it will be like at sea. There is no raid. I am alone with my thoughts.

Five years ago, I had a plan. I was going to write my page every week in the *Sunday Express* and then at the end of that time go off round the world in search of new experience, that well of experience from which a writer must draw all the time, and must constantly refill or perish.

Honolulu. Mexico. South Africa. Hollywood. They were names that I had often recited softly to myself in days of peace. A kind of mirage of escape. Was Sydney Harbour finer than the entrance to Rio in the dawn? I would find that out one day.

But something intervened. And now instead of crossing to America in the *Queen Mary* or the *Normandie*, I am just off instead to sea again in a ship so small in comparison that you would have hardly noticed it from the promenade decks of those great liners. However, instead of paying for my passage, I shall be the privileged guest of men who in the years when peace returns again, we can never repay sufficiently for the part they are playing in keeping our sea lines of communication open and free. And it is because they never ask anything in return, that I am devoting all the royalties which accrue from the sale of this book to the King George Fund for Sailors. I am afraid that the gift is very inadequate, for it would be impossible ever to repay all the kindness and the understanding and the hospitality that I have received " somewhere out there."

Somewhere out there. . . . Sometimes I think I am crazy to be so keen to get back once again into the Battle

7

of the Atlantic. Obviously I am in for a tough trip and yet rather to my surprise I must confess my mind, as I sit now at my desk, is filled with a great sense of exultation, because—and I think this is important and worth recording since it concerns so many other members of my generation beside myself—I am having in this war a real chance at last to get to grips with real things and real people.

Some people are fond of quoting the phrase, " the eternal verities." I don't like abstract phrases very much myself. Do you? Anyway, let's put it another way. The war has taught us all—at least it should have taught us—that a man goes to his destiny and therefore it is foolish to be afraid of death ; that the accident of death is so unimportant beside the purpose of living—of living each day to the full, because you do not know what to-morrow may bring forth ; and being able to say truthfully and fearlessly that it does not matter what may happen to you, because, after all, you have *lived*.

Always in the years, the uneasy years of the botched peace, those who like myself were only small children in the last war felt a crippling barrier between ourselves and that other generation, the generation who had been prepared to sacrifice everything that we might live.

Do you remember the inscription on the Unknown Warrior's tomb? " *They buried him among the kings because he had done good towards God and towards His house.*" They were inside that sacred circle ; we outside, right outside. And nothing that we could do then could break down the barriers. Let it be admitted that some of us did not even want to, were content to be dismissed as selfish, self-seeking, soft. While in return, in self-defence, we would secretly call them bores when they spoke of the Somme and Jutland and Passchendaele. May God forgive us.

He has forgiven us, praise be. He has given us the chance to-day to prove that after all we were a generation worth saving, worth fighting for, that in our regenerated bones and in our blood is the same mixture that could make a paradise out of hell during those four long years for comrades in arms. That comradeship we were once so bitterly outside.

To-day that paradise still exists for all of us, equally, in the front line. That is the wonder of it. But it is also the truth. It takes strange forms. You will find it, as I have found it, under the parapet of an Ack-Ack gun site, where the only bed for the men to rest on between bouts of standing-to is a bed of shells waiting to be loaded ; in an A.F.S. sub-station, where women ambulance drivers and men stretcher-bearers, dressed alike in trousers, play cards together as they wait for their names to go up on the board, knowing and accepting the fact that their chances outside in the blitz are fair and equal. In an office, any office like ours, for instance, high up under the sky, when I have gone into my Editor's room on a Saturday morning during the Battle for Britain, and found him serenely writing away at his desk something which had to be written, with a very necessary tin hat on his head to which neither of us referred.

Am I talking through my own hat, did I exaggerate when I called it a paradise, even with a small p ? It is for you to decide from your own experience when you have finished turning over the chapters of this front-line diary, but surely you must agree that though the war, which we all dreaded in Munich days, is every bit as foul and beastly and heart-rending in its wanton destruction as the prophets warned us, yet it produces compensations that we never suspected.

It has given a generation back its manhood. It has restored youth to a generation who imagined that they were already middle-aged, and now in the Home Guards, as roof spotters, back at sea again, perceive that it is simply that they were tired from too great a weight of weary dis-illusionment. Finally it has given women the opportunity and the proud privilege they never possessed in the last war, of sharing danger and discomfort equally with their menfolk, and emerging from the ordeal with equally positive proof, were any needed, of the innate courage of their sex.

And something else has emerged besides the courage of

which it is a commonplace to write, and that is the spark of nobility, immortality, call it what you like, which separates us from the beasts of the field. Every time I go to sea again, I am struck once more by the depth of instinctive religious feeling of those who have spent their lives in ships; whereas on the shore, I have been often assailed since the war by the argument: How can you believe in a God who allows war to return again and again?

What is the answer to that? I've only five minutes left before I must go and catch my train. I feel an urgency to write down now, before it is too late, something that has been in my mind a long time, something that I believe myself with all my heart and mind.

Nearly two thousand years ago, Christ died a more horrible death than any raid disaster. But what is two thousand years in the history of the world? It is simply a comma in that sentence called eternity. Surely He died . . . as men died in the last war . . . as men and women are dying to-day . . . to prove that such things as unselfishness and nobility and altruism are more important and always will be, than the false wooden gods set up by tyrants.

It may take more than another two thousand years to prove that with finality. But meanwhile, look around you. Who would deny that there are more people trying to live like Christ to-day than ever in this country before? Think of the folk who have stuck it out in the East End, Plymouth, Bristol, Coventry, Hull and Newcastle. Merseyside and Clydeside. The list is endless. Isn't there something Christ-like in their acceptance of their lot? Something Christlike in the way that every one, yes every one, has become a better neighbour to-day, and all barriers between communities down at last?

And that is why, out again in the Atlantic once more, sick as a dog as I always am, yet I know that I shall feel happier and more at peace than ever in my life before. And if this special prologue to this book were the last thing that I ever wrote, I should be content.

GODFREY WINN.

CONTENTS

ACT ONE

ACT TWO

LIST OF ILLUSTRATIONS

Act One

Chapter One

ATLANTIC SHEEPDOG

ABOVE the mantelpiece of the Operations Room at the Base, there hung a joke-sketch of an Extraordinary mass meeting of the Stragglers Club. A famous Naval caricaturist had drawn a picture of two or three boatloads of irate survivors, shaking their fists at each other and arguing as to whose fault it was. The Base Commander smiled : "It's the stragglers who always get caught," he said. "You're going with your convoy bang into the fun. You should get Focke-Wulfs by day, submarines by night. Good hunting to you."

From somewhere down the street, an out-of-tune piano was playing the "Londonderry Air." I had never realized before what a sad tune it could be. On our way towards the port, we passed a long line of sailors queueing up for a free Sunday night's cinema show. They were laughing and whistling at the girls who, in decorous couples, walked by on the other side of the street. Our last evening ashore.

We sailed early in the morning to our rendezvous. A giant convoy. As we went down the line, the captain of our corvette held the Ardente speaker, like a microphone, to his lips. Each ship received the same message. "*Close up before dark. Fear of enemy attack.*" In harsh, warning eddies of sound, his roughly amplified voice disturbed the stillness of the spring evening.

I stood on the bridge and looked at the captain's list of the convoy. There were ships, I found, bound for all the four corners of the earth. Would they ever reach their many destinations ? As though they could sense what was in my mind, someone in the bridgehouse said : "You only hear about the convoys that are attacked, seldom about the millions of tons of stuff that gets through." Thanks to ships like yours, I thought.

I was proud to be sailing in that corvette, for she was the first one of this new class of vessel to be commissioned and launched, and ever since, she had been keeping ceaseless guard over countless convoys, dropping her depth charges whenever she got contact through her Asdic apparatus with a U-boat. Many times she had gone through the fire to pick up survivors from a blazing tanker, on her stern there was the mark where a torpedo had grazed her side ; but Arthur, the Number One Asdic rating, wore the D.S.M. for the last submarine they had bagged. Convoy in and convoy out, they had ridden the storm.

You sense the atmosphere of a ship, like that of a town, the moment you set foot in her. Our corvette, with her crew of sixty, her four officers, her packed accommodation, so that the men richly deserve their hard-lying money, reminded me at once of a little Northern mining town. Dour and isolated and prepared always for the worst, with nothing to spend on idle emotion, but nothing, either, to surrender in loyalty or spirit.

How did you celebrate your bag of a submarine? I asked in the wardroom the first night out. We couldn't celebrate at sea, I was told. For days at a time, in rough weather, they can't reach us from the galley, we live on biscuits and bully beef. By the time we got back to shore, it seemed too far away.

Number One, who was speaking, was busy meshing a net tied by one end to the pole which supported the centre of the wardroom. It was his idea, next time we dropped a depth charge, to catch from the stern any fish that came stunned and floating to the surface. Fresh fish at sea. The greatest luxury of all.

Trump, the steward, who used to play Rugger for the Navy, grinned and continued his methodical ministrations. He'd had a brain-wave, too. In order to prevent all the plates cascading off the table, he produced a cupful of water, and dipping his fingers into it, he damped the cloth

(*Above*) Corvettes are notorious in the Service for their corkscrew roll ;
corkscrew because they never roll twice in the same way.

(*Below*) The only coins that have any value on board are those of guts,
good comradeship and a sense of humour.

all round. I used to watch him before every meal that I wasn't going to eat. All that water outside, I used to think, nothing but sea and more sea, and now Trump with his patent device. But it worked. By some miracle, the crockery did stay on the wardroom table.

The wardroom was barren, airless, uncomfortable. There were no pictures on the wall as you would find in a destroyer's mess, not even as a mascot a coloured drawing of the sturdy little white rock flower from which our corvette took its name. All the corvettes are called after flowers. I wonder why, I used to think as I lay awake night after night dossed down on the wardroom seat for a bunk. If you roll off, you'll only roll into the table, the captain said.

Corvettes are notorious in the Service for their cork-screw roll ; corkscrew, because they never roll twice in the same way. However, it is a considerable consolation to open your eyes from time to time and see what is happening to some of the smaller ships in the convoy all round you. Their bows right out of the water, puffing and blowing they are to keep up, and our corvette at intervals through the day chases round their tails, like a sheepdog with a flock on its way to market. Even so, there is the inevitable straggler who won't keep her position. . . . But you see how she'll put on steam when the attack comes, someone prophesied.

That was not until the fifth afternoon out. Or was it the fifth month? Ninety per cent monotony and discomfort, ten per cent excitement and action, that's how they describe their life. Beside the guardian corvettes, guardian aircraft made a pattern, too, round the convoy. Round and round all day long, until you were giddy watching, because there was nothing else to watch, except the toy balloons, like a kid plays with on the heath, floating incongruously in the wake of some of the ships.

But *he* goes home every night in his aeroplane, lucky beggar, exclaimed the signalman on the bridge beside me, who at the beginning of the war had been in a printing works at Loughborough and had as his last job, ironically, the printing of three million Navy leave tickets. He goes home every night . . . he repeated, wistfully.

The boy who had just come down from keeping the look-out watch in the crow's nest, his cheeks as blue from cold as his balaclava, picked up the last sentence. Home. Ever been to Wigan? he asked me. Before I could answer, he continued : "Some say it's only a small place, and others that it's a dirty town. But to me, it's the most beautiful spot in the world. And we haven't lost a Rugger match this season. I hope to see them play next Saturday. We're going on boiler leave after this trip."

If you're lucky, I thought . . . and at that moment, through the length of the ship rang the three sharp piercing bells, which is the signal for Submarine Action Stations. And in the same split second, from somewhere ahead, there came the repercussion of depth charges, shaking our corvette, like a heavy chain being dragged beneath our keel.

I glanced to the left and there was the straggler, as though someone had suddenly given it a kick in the pants, shooting forward with a great wash at its stern, and I laughed to see the sudden turn of speed that it could produce after all, and dashed into the bridgehouse to hear the messages coming through on the R.T.—(radio telephone)—from the destroyer in charge of the convoy.

Just below us, one of the gun crews was assembled, looking in their hooded duffle coats like a party of the Klu Klux Klan, and their shells in a semi-circle round them, each one tilted slightly on a separate stand, reminded me suddenly of vintage bottles of port, laid out preciously on their sides in a fabulous cellar. And I laughed again at the thoughts which come to your mind at such a moment.

H—— has dropped depth charges on firm contact. . . . The voice through the R.T. is like the sports master at your prep. school, bawling at you patiently to line up now on Sports Day for the last race of the afternoon.

Our captain was running his own race, he wore grey flannel bags and slippers, a beret and the top part of Army battle dress dyed blue-black which he had acquired in

Iceland. Round and round the narrow bridge he pattered, mad keen to get into the fight, you could see the saliva on his lips at the thought of the hunt, at the realization of what those depth charges meant. The bag, the kill.

Depth charges cost forty quid each. I was trying to do the sum in my head, thinking whatever the cost, it was worth it to save a convoy, and then again the R.T. blotted out everything else in one's mind. The same polite, unhurried tones, and now the message was : *The gunnery officer of M—— has just reported seeing the bows of the submarine in the middle of the convoy.*

I thought our captain would have a fit, he was so excited. And when the last laconic message came " *Off hunting,*" I felt quite sorry for him ; he had wanted to be in at the death so much, but our job was to stay and protect the convoy on this occasion. Several more days and nights before at last the signal to turn round, which is a signal, too, for every one to shave for the first time since we left harbour.

That night we celebrated our coming return by a game of whist in the mess deck. You play for the love of the companionship, the laugh that goes up when " Guns " gets ragged for not returning his partner's lead, the sense of security as the cards are dealt hand after hand, as though instead of all the creaking and groaning and muffled cries of the ship, hundreds of miles out there in the Atlantic, you will hear the rat-a-tat-tat of the postman as he passes down the street, or the slam of the letter-box as the paper boy pushes through the Sunday papers.

Late, I came out on to the boat deck and stood by the rails for a moment before dossing down in the wardroom. The moon rode high and full and the silhouettes of the convoy looked as though they had been cut out of tinfoil. A shadow moved a few feet away and I recognized Arthur, our Asdic expert. He was gazing at something, holding it towards the light of the moon. " What's that you've got, Arthur ? " I asked. " Oh, it's my bit of misery," he replied.

Shyly, he put it into my hand and I saw that the piece of cardboard was the picture of a very beautiful girl. " My wife," he said   And on his face there shone a look of beatitude I shall never forget, more dazzling than the moon.

Very early next morning, we left the convoy and at the last moment, perversely, I was sorry to turn round, though we had talked of nothing else for days. Suddenly the smoke from the little coalers seemed so matey and when the last black splodge vanished over the horizon, my hopes went with them.

And now the Atlantic seemed overwhelmingly large and lonely again. I looked out across the grey waste and discovered, about a quarter of a mile away, another ship riding to starboard of us. What on earth's that tiny little boat doing here? I asked. "Don't be a damn fool," they said. "That's another corvette. It's exactly the same size as we are."

The two corvettes came home together for company, and somehow just as a dog instinctively seems to sense when you are homeward bound and starts to quicken its pace, so did our corvette seem to move more swiftly through the water.

I was sitting on a barrel on the boat deck one morning —at least, not sitting so much as squatting with my eyes shut to blot out the swell that was breaking over us, when suddenly I was hailed and there was Tanky standing beside me.

Tanky is the name on every small vessel for the ship's butcher. Actually, we had long since ceased to have any fresh provisions. It was bully beef, bully beef all the time now, though the evening we attacked the submarine, we celebrated our victory by calling it Sea Horse Pie, for a change, which is like our Shepherd's Pie on shore—minced meat at the bottom and potato on top, and the sailors put a particular crinkly crust of waves to justify its name.

"Have a drop of Nelson's blood," Tanky was saying, as he held out towards me a spotless wine-glass. I can't imagine where he'd got it from, and the contrast with Tanky himself in his filthy overalls, his orange whiskers, and ancient green tam o' shanter, was something you would remember always. In the glass there was a brown-red mixture and I suddenly realized that Tanky was offering me his daily tot of rum, more precious to him than anything else on board. Could hospitality go further than that?

When I shook my head, he added: "Anyway, I shouldn't sit on that barrel, chum . . . do you know what it is . . . it's a depth charge." I got up as quickly as though a Focke-Wulf had dropped an egg on the deck behind me. We leant together over the rails, and my companion went on talking, almost to himself. " I wonder if any one got it last night," he said. " I hope it wasn't London, because my missus has been bombed out of two homes already. But she won't budge. She says, if I can take it out at sea, she can take it on shore. He'll never beat the women, will he?"

Again I shook my head, and he continued: " It's funny, you know, how out at sea you think things out. I suppose it's because you've got so much time on your hands. I reckon myself that if a fellow hangs on long enough, it does come out all right in the end. Look at old Haile Selassie. Do you know, I was in the cruiser, *Enterprise* it was, that took him off from Jibuti, with his family and two hundred and seventy boxes of gold and silver. You never saw such a how-d'ye-do. The kids got lost and were finally discovered gorging themselves in the canteen with the troops. On our way up the Red Sea, we passed two Italian transports going the other way. The soldiers lined the rails and laughed and grimaced at us. They knew who we'd got on board. Well, I should think the Italians in Abyssinia are laughing on the other side of their face now, and the old boy back in triumph in his capital. That's what I'd have liked to have seen."

At that moment, the coxswain comes by and in his hand he holds a copper jug. Empty. It is his privilege each morning at eleven to dish out the ration of Nelson's Blood, now poured down the throats of our sixty crew. He stops by the rail, too, and asks me if I ever met Lord Jellicoe.

This time I nod, having a memory of a week-end when I was staying in the same house and a quiet, little old gentleman played bridge and sat in a corner, never venturing an opinion, and yet somehow dominating the whole party, despite his deafness and his shortness of stature.

The coxswain is talking : " Twenty-six years I've been in the Service. I served as a boy in the *Iron Duke* in the last war, and I shall never forget the day that Jellicoe left us. Three times his admiral's barge circled the ship in farewell, while we all stood to attention on deck, and you can take it from me, sir, there wasn't a dry eye among us. We loved him to a man as he loved us."

And as he spoke, you had an extraordinary sense of the perpetuity of the pattern, of the way that great ships like the *Iron Duke* and small ships like the corvette in which I was sailing, fit together into that pattern, because of the tradition handed down by Drake and Nelson and carried on by such men as the coxswain standing beside me, who was not ashamed to speak of his devotion for officers like Jellicoe who have made the Service what it is to-day.

Down in the wardroom that night, they were discussing the latest class of battleship, the *King George V.*, and they were telling me how when Lord Halifax crossed to America in her, the captain invited him to read the lessons at Sunday morning prayers. And they told me, too, of the party given ashore when they berthed safely, by the Naval Academy at Annapolis, where apparently lies the only White Ensign ever captured. That was in the frigate action of 1812. But our boys weren't shown it that night at the party, because their hosts were doubtless afraid that in a sortie they would lose their prize ! Incidentally, the Academy is dry. And I understand our fellows had the spectacle of seeing hundreds of snotties at their supper, tossing down glasses of milk.

We ourselves were drinking lime juice. Bottles and bottles of it we drank on the voyage home. And we raised our glasses silently in what may seem rather a strange toast. *By the grace of God and British fortitude.* But it may not seem so strange when I tell you whence it came. The logbook of the first officer of a ship torpedoed somewhere out in the Atlantic a few months ago.

The only two survivors were thrown up on the beach of one of the islands in the Bahamas. You may have read their story, but nothing in that story can compare with one single entry from the logbook that was washed up with them, all that is left of the memory of the men who, tortured by thirst and defenceless to the sun, were compelled one by one to surrender to the sea. But still on the twenty-eighth day in that open boat, the first officer had the courage and the faith to write: "Hope to make a landfall this evening by the Grace of God and British fortitude."

You might remember those words. I lay awake with them for company, after our snotty has gone to keep the middle watch and the captain has gone to his cabin and the lights are out, and I am dossing down on the wardroom seat once more. The ship is full of strange creaks. The bilge pumps make a curious, disembodied sound as though all the souls of all the drowned were crying out to be revenged.

You cannot sleep for the rolling, and you start thinking of other convoys not so lucky as yours: of the story you have been told that night of an attack, when in the darkness they saw the company of one of the torpedoed ships, with their faces upturned in the water towards the moon. They looked like a host of lascars, and then suddenly above the sound of the wind they heard the scream of a woman, and realized that what they had mistaken for the skin of a lascar was really the oil from the explosion. And they themselves were helpless, because when they threw down ropes, the life-lines slipped through their hands, with the casing of oil. And as you think of that, once again the bilge pumps make their moaning, tortured cry.

But next morning when you go up on the bridge, the sun is shining, the nightmare is forgotten. And there is Tanky with his wineglass full of rum again. But not for me this time, but for a Manx lad who is celebrating his twenty-first birthday. There is a little group round him, including a fellow who has come all the way from New Zealand to help win the Battle of the Atlantic. What are the girls like on the Isle of Man? he asks. The boy grins and turned to me and says, as he drinks up his Nelson's Blood : " From now on I have the key of the door."

He means that there is a custom on his island that when you come of age, you are given the key of the front door, but to me it has a much deeper and wider significance than that. The long voyage home is coming to an end. I have seen a convoy guarded to safety and a submarine which attacked us sent to the bottom of the ocean. I have seen men with their ear against the wireless set thousands of miles out at sea, trying to catch the news from home, simply to find out how their own home-town has been faring.

But the rest of the war news has meant little to them. They have their own job to do and they are doing it. And that is why the key to the door is in their hand, why we shall win the Battle of the Atlantic in the end. By the grace of God and British fortitude. . . .

Chapter Two

SUBMARINE SILHOUETTE

THE LIGHT was beginning to fade from the hills and the loch was very still. I stood beside the rail of the depot ship for submarines whose guest I was, whither they return from their patrols for replenishment and rest. Here their " tube," as they call their submarine, is refilled with stores and fresh " fish " are placed upon the torpedo racks in the bows, and the crew come on board the mother-ship and luxuriate for a long time in a hot bath, having unpeeled their clothes for the first time for many weeks. While if they like, they can have sun-ray treatment in the sick-bay and go ashore to stretch their legs. After every other patrol, they have leave. Does any branch of any Service deserve it more?

So I was thinking as I stood beside the rail and watched. For it is from here, too, that they go forth again on patrol as soon as their boat is ready. One submarine is going now. Look, the Ensign flutters from her bridge, above the recogtion flags. It catches the last of the daylight, whiter than the jerseys of some of the crew who line the side. They do not salute as she glides away from her moorings beside her fellow " tubes." The only movement comes from the captain on the bridge, who makes the thumbs-up gesture familiar to the R.A.F. There are no cheers for her previous successes. This is a moment of silent speculation, secret exhortation.

Beside me on the quarterdeck were the men whose turn it will be to sail to-morrow and to-morrow. What is in their minds? What is the make-up of a submariner? Come with me on board one of their " tubes." It belongs to the latest class, infinitely superior to anything the Germans possess. About two hundred and seventy feet long, she has a displacement of 1300 tons. Once upon a time, to write of such statistics would have seemed dull to me, but think what it must be like never to be able to take, for weeks on end, more than 270 steps, one way or the other.

And width? Well, there is one narrow passage which goes the length of the boat from the torpedoes in the bows to the " Dead End kids," the stokers in the stern. It is no wider than the corridor of a train, so that two men have difficulty in passing each other and one will step aside into a mess's alcove. For the size of each mess is hardly larger than the cubicle in a hairdressing shop, where women have their hair permanently waved. Perhaps you think of that comparison, because there is a curtain across the aperture and there are five of them in a row, scattered down the length of the boat. Next to the torpedoes live the seamen and then the P.O.s, and then the E.R.A.s (We run the ship, said the engine room artificers in chorus, but the petty officers say the same, so what !) and then the wardroom, and next to it, the only separate cabin in the ship, where the captain sleeps on top of the Control Room, which must dominate his sleeping as well as his waking hours. And finally, the " Dead End kids " again.

Two hours on and four hours off. Two hours on and four hours off. Work, eat, sleep ; work, eat, sleep. You can repeat aloud the routine a dozen times and you can only capture a semblance of the monotony of the reality. From the moment that they set out on patrol to the moment when they return, three-quarters of the sixty crew never see the light of day, or rather the feel of the night air upon their faces, when after dusk, the " tube " surfaces and recharges her batteries.

Out on patrol, they have their main meal at night. And they have their hot dinner at that hour, because when the submarine is on the surface, cold reviving air percolates through the conning tower and sweeps down the passages and into their lungs and the heaviness goes from their heads and their appetite returns.

We don't talk much, they told me, except just after we've been issued with our daily tot of rum. And they don't write letters until the last day of the patrol, and they don't read much, either, but just sit in their mess, between sleeping and eating, and stare up at the silhouettes of the pretty ladies that they have cut out from magazines and stuck over their lockers.

How do you like our art gallery ? they ask you. It is something to look at and to remind you of the touch of life when you are lying as silent as the grave at the bottom of the ocean, drifting two knots, as you seek to escape from the depth charges reverberating around you with a dull plomp, plomp sound. (Lucky if it is only that and not right on top of you and the lights fusing amid the crashing of crockery. When that happened on one occasion in the Skaggerak, I found myself saying to my steward : " More coffee, Allenby, more coffee, Allenby," one commander told me.)

When they know you better, they show you something else—how, from pieces of brass, they carve exquisite little models of their " tube " in silhouette. On their return, and it is a kind of talisman against their return, they go ashore and have them dipped in silver for their wife, whose picture is over their bunk. One boy, " Taffy," from Bridgend, had just returned from four days' special leave to be married. And he asked me to write to his wife to tell her not to worry if she does not hear from him now for some little time.

On the last night before they sailed, they taught me how to play poker dice. See if you can get five Aces in your first throw, they challenged me. I got five Jacks instead. They were just as pleased. They took it as an omen.

Submariners call the area of their patrol, their " billet." Rather surprisingly, the time they like least during their patrol is on their way out to the " billet " and on their way back again. In the depot ship, I was privileged to be shown, in the operations room, the plotting flags on the great map which shows the " billets " of all our submarines. For obvious reasons, I cannot betray the secrets of my privileged visit, but I can assure you that the numbers given by the Germans as to the flotillas they have at sea at present come into the same category as the monstrous lies they produce of our shipping losses. They take a number and multiply it forty times over. Incidentally, it is reckoned that it needs four submarines to keep one at sea, just as it is supposed to take forty men to get an aeroplane off the ground. You see, there is the submarine on patrol, the one on its way to relieve it, the one on its way back and the one in dock being refuelled and overhauled.

The doctor on the depot ship told me that after their first patrol, submariners usually have lost weight ; subsequently, however, they usually put it on. Perhaps this is due to the fact that, in the last few months, a revolution in catering has taken place. Now, in a two-pound tin, are stored sufficient fresh vegetables for one hundred and sixty men. You don't believe me? I didn't believe it myself at first when they showed me the tin full of what appeared to be dried grass. That was cabbage! Spinach! And then from another tin they gave me what I thought was a piece of straw. They assured me it was worth its weight in gold and I tasted it and realized, the next second, that I was eating sufficient compressed onions for a dozen men? and I wasn't allowed to forget that for the rest of the day.

The revolution comes from Canada. The vegetables are dehydrated. That means that by a vacuum process, all the moisture is drawn away from the vegetables which, when they are placed in boiling water for half an hour, expand to their former cubic capacity, and then can be cooked in the normal way. The name of the firm is an Ontario one, Beardmore. I should think our submarine crews will bless the name for evermore.

Menus for each patrol are worked out in detail in the depot ship. Here, for example, are the meals for the last day of the fifth week. For breakfast, grape fruit, herrings in tomato sauce. For dinner, soup, veal and ham galantine, apples and custard. For tea, syrup. For supper, actually eaten at the time when most of us have our lunch, stewed tinned steak, boiled potatoes, carrots, fruit pie and cocoa. Instead of the various submarines doing their own buying from the canteen, the mother-ship takes over all the catering and by clever purchases in the wholesale market, has succeeded in bringing down messing to 2s. 5½d. a day.

Submarine crews, like the R.A.F., have their own slang. When they are fed up, everything is "threadbare." All the same, they make a joke of not being able to spend anything on board, and their pay, with their danger money, works out at about eight shillings a day for seamen. There are jars of boiled sweets in every mess, because they cannot smoke when their "tube" is submerged. All the same, when they play "Hearts," they play for a cigarette a hand.

Pretend you are sitting with me in the mess now, where the captain has just said, with a deprecatory smile : " That's my only claim to fame, I am afraid. I won 187 cigarettes on our last patrol."

You glance at his tunic and on it are the ribbons of the D.S.O. and the D.S.C. Before he sets off on patrol again, he will have to visit London and Buckingham Palace for the investiture. His fellow officers in the wardroom all express the hope that there will be a picture in the papers. My wife's bought a new hat, the captain adds. It is always of someone else he wishes to speak, never of himself or his exploits.

As I was saying good-bye, he asked me to pass on a message. I expected some stirring call to harder work on the home front. But these men are too modest, too self-effacing to make such demands. Instead, all he said was : " By the way, there is something we awfully want for our ' tube,' if you could get hold of one." " What is it ? " The answer was unexpected : " One of those motor horns that play a tune when you press them." I have been searching for one ever since. . . .

I had the thrill of hearing the horn they have now, just inside the conning tower, which the officer on the watch presses to warn the ship's company to go to diving stations. How that familiar street-sound must quicken the beat of their hearts, for submariners on leave. I know that it quickened mine when they re-enacted for me one of their most successful recent attacks.

Imagine a moonless night, and suddenly two hundred and fifty yards away the officer on watch sees another submarine come to the surface. Instantly, the order to submerge. The look-outs are rushing past me down the conning tower. Then myself, and then bringing up the rear the Number One, who as he slid down the narrow steps, sounded the horn and closed the top hatch, all in one motion.

As they went through the exact motion of submerging

for me, I was struck most of all by the silence. The busy silence, one called it afterwards, and assured me that it is always the same. Another said it's like a silent film. Those tiny sounds, inside the " tube," but nothing without. No sound of surging waters, no pressure of submersion.

Down in the control room, there are a dozen members of the crew at their stations, around us. We are submerging at the rate of one foot a second. The periscope is being wound up through the floor, and the captain, who told me that they preferred a target at 800-1000 feet—this is point-blank range—is peering through the periscope with an old jacket over his head, unconsciously using the same pose as the family album photographer of Victorian days.

Then with the periscope just out of the water, he gives the order : Steady. Fire. A second later, a great explosion shook the submarine like a host of depth charges on top. When the repercussion had died away and they came to the surface, the enemy was gone and the sea was as still as though the attack had never been. But now, on the conning tower, are painted five grey chevrons, which stand for five successes gained in six patrols by the expenditure of eight torpedoes. Cold figures that warm your heart.

Add to that German submarine, an Italian one. Add a tanker. And two supply ships. And add something else, too. Looking down upon the trot of submarines, still left beside the mother-ship, my companion said, as together we watched the patrol go out : " You see, it's more difficult for us, because the Germans have their targets given them on a plate. We have to go a long way to find ours."

Yes, a long way, I thought, suddenly noticing a cold wind coming off the hills. Now the last flicker of white from the Ensign is disappearing round the far bend of the loch and we turn from the rails and go back into the ward-room and have a " Horse's Neck."

Chapter Three

NO TIME TO GRAB A HARP

IF anything should touch us now, you wouldn't have time to grab a harp, he exclaimed, almost under his breath, in that silent, sweating moment of gathering tension. I did not answer. There is no answer when you are pressed up close to the unrailed stern of a minelayer, just about to operate and cast overboard its cargo of " eggs," as the crew call them, each weighing half a ton.

It is pitch dark, surely darker even than the other place where they do not hand out harps. With your back to the sea, looking away into the illimitable cavern where the cargo, in four rows, two on the starboard side, two on the port side, is housed against this moment, you cannot distinguish which shapes are men at their action stations, which the mines, attached to their sinkers. You can only hear instead, from somewhere the other end of the tunnel, the first snatches of the song the crew always sing as they wait for the shaded light to flash its signal, when the captain on the bridge is satisfied that we are over the exact spot in the minefield we are laying.

This is the song :

" Bless 'em all, bless 'em all,
    You get no promotion this side of the ocean,
    So cheer up my lads . . . bless 'em all."

Earlier in the wardroom, my companion by the starboard winch, the ship's Torpedo Gunner, who had retired after the last war to grow cabbages as he thought, had confessed to me : You know, going back to sea at fifty-two, you don't feel as young as you did. Well, I must confess I did not feel particularly young myself at that moment, remembering, every time the ship gave a lurch, how close we were to the last line of mines that our ship had despatched over the stern a few nights before.

Earlier again in the afternoon, I had watched him carefully pull on a pair of stiff gardening gloves, such as my mother wears to prune the roses and keep out thorns. But we are a long way from the garden of our cottage, even from the early spring sunshine washing the decks above. For we are in the tunnelled bowels of the ship, reminiscent of an Underground railway with its twin tracks, and we are watching the gunner pass from mine to mine, with their wicked horns—let any ship touch one of those beneath the water—and proceed to fix inside the primer and the detonator, which make them henceforth dangerous and deadly weapons of war.

As the gunner and the team working with him passed on down the row, I suddenly had a flash-back to the first time I saw the pantomime of Ali Baba and the Forty Thieves, for the shining black mines, standing on their sinkers, might just as well have been the barrels of oil in that mythical cave. When I suggested that to one of the crew—the ship has a complement of seventy men and five officers—this was his reply : If Old Nasty and his boy friend Musso were hiding in them now, they'd get more than a dose of boiling oil . . . bless 'em all. Whereupon he gave the side of the mine an affectionate pat !

I knew what was really in the mines, because on shore I had watched the process of their filling at the depot. They had shown me a barrel full of what I mistook at first for golden chaff or oatmeal. In reality, it was deadly T.N.T., which is mixed with ammonia nitrate, and the result when it is poured into the mine, still looks as harmless as golden syrup.

Some of the barrels were a consignment from overseas, and in one of them recently, amid the " grain," they unearthed a dead mouse side by side with a snake. They think that the snake must have pursued the mouse into the barrel in search of a meal. And then, mistaken the T.N.T., and gorged itself and died. Anyway, when they showed me the preserved remains, I could not help thinking that the Nazis represented the snake, who had mistaken us for

Now take care and see that next time you don't have to walk back through the Drink, they exclaim in chorus.

a mouse, a mouse that has turned into a lion once again and is still very much alive.

Just as the boys on our minelayer were very much alive, too, though their unchanging routine is perhaps the most dangerous of all jobs performed at sea to-day, yes, worse even than the life on a minesweeper, but it is impossible for them to receive the recognition they deserve, because their work must be performed in such complete secrecy. But this can be put on record. The minelayer in which I sailed was the first ship to go out on operations, two hours after declaration of war, and on our trip cast upon the waters its three thousand five hundredth mine.

Now as I write to-night, safely on shore again, I know that my new friends are out again at sea, and despite everything, I wish I were back in the mess deck, filling in the time before zero hour, playing darts and pontoon with Harry from Pompey, and his mates. Very mild gambling, but believe me, far more thrilling than the high table at Monte Carlo. Give him a clod, keep your snow, advised Harry. A clod is a copper. Snow is silver, a threepenny bit in this case.

Farther along the table, other fellows are writing letters home. Each one of them has the same-sized attaché case open in front of them. It is a Navy issue. In this he keeps all his private letters and most precious possessions. Snapshots, such as the ones I am so proud to have the chance to reproduce in this book. And they have universally turned the lids of each of the cases into a kind of family picture gallery, with photographs of their mothers and their dogs and the girl friend, of course. One of the boys who is writing away page after page is sending a letter to Abbey Wood, S.E.2. Tom has a round, unlined, trusting face. He started life behind a counter in Regent Street. But it was too dull for me, he says ; I wanted a bit of adventure. Well, he's getting that all right now. When the minelaying commences, he is No. 1 starboard trap.

That means it is his job to stand closest to the water's

edge and release the spring which allows each mine to go forward and topple over into the sea. It is he who literally pushes it on its way. And if the safety device, which is supposed to prevent it going off during the first thirty-five seconds it is submerged, did not function, and accidents happen in the best regulated mines, then it would be Tom who would be nearest the explosion. But you would never guess that from his serene smile as he bends over his writing pad.

Next door to Tom is a fellow who clearly, a few days previously, must have put forward a request to " grow." What do I mean by that ? Well, look on the notice board of Number 5 Mess, and there you will read :

" Since the Requests to ' Grow ' were approved, sufficient time has passed to indicate those who have ' reasonable possibilities.' Although ' personal pride of possession ' might make some of the triers unprepared to admit the fact, it is obvious to those without interest in the matter that the majority of the attempts are abject failures and nothing but disfiguring growths. The attempt to ' GROW ' will not be accepted as an excuse for untidyness or unkemptness, therefore from to-morrow, Monday, all ratings are to be CLEAN SHAVEN or have NEAT TRIMMED BEARDS."

Incidentally, our captain served in the last war with the present C.-in-C. of the Mediterranean Fleet and told me the story of how on one occasion, his steward asked Commander Cunningham, as he then was, whether he should buy him a comb when he went on shore. Nonsense, replied the commander, I never grow my hair long enough to need a comb.

That certainly went for some of the beards on board, although there were so many attempts to ' grow ' that I was reminded of a submarine crew. Other similarities, too. Inevitably, so much space on the ship has to be given up to the housing of the mines themselves, that in consequence the men's quarters are very restricted, while their portholes cannot be opened since they are right up against the waterline.

Wherefore the crew feel that they deserve " hard lying money." That works out at about another sixpence a day pay. Now on all these trips, I am simply a messenger who watches, listens and records. But it struck me as typical of the spirit right through the Service that I have never once heard the crew make any complaint about the constant danger they are in from an accident to the " eggs " before they are safely overboard, but instead, all their grouses—and all good sailors, like all good soldiers, grouse —concerned the fact that there was not sufficient room to swing their hammocks.

The cards are put away, the game is over, I continue on my way. In half an hour's time, it will be zero hour. As I come up the companionway, I look in on Sparks, who hails from West Hartlepool, and has been presented with three sets of twins by his wife, who was herself a twin. Is this a record ? Anyway, Sparks is still hoping to set up one.

Up above on the bridge, Alan, one of the subs., helps me get my bearings in the darkness. The ship itself is trying to get its bearings, too, measuring the distance from a fixed sea-mark, by the aid of gear wire, which can give us our position, on a certain arc, down to the last foot. You can imagine how important it is that we should start laying on the right spot, because of the other minefields close at hand.

The sub. and I come from the same home town. He, too, was born and brought up just outside Birmingham and he has been telling me about one of his ship's recent voyages when they laid mines right up against enemy occupied territory. They watched the searchlights seeking their prey, the arcs of betraying light just missed their bows as they went in, closer and closer to the coast. Twenty minutes and their job was over and they just succeeded in getting out again with the searchlight passing their stern this time by a few precious feet.

Now he suddenly breaks the silence to exclaim as we wait for the captain to give the signal—Stand by to lay mines—I wouldn't mind being in Corporation Street or New Street this moment, would you, Godfrey? No, Alan, I wouldn't. Funny how grubby, prosaic, sooty Brum, should be transformed into a picture of paradise for both of us. . . .

All the same, I don't think you would have thought that funny had you been crouching beside me up against the gear in the stern, waiting and watching. We are back again at the beginning of the story. Look, there it goes, the light is flashing. We're off.

Instinctively, you take a deep breath as Tom, now a smudge in the darkness, releases his gear and the first mine slides forward. The process of submersion is the same as with a human being who, diving head foremost into the water, comes up again still head first. I look back over my shoulder, into the wake of the mine, watching it disappear in the phosphorescent water, with its sinker attached to it. Down, down, at twenty feet a second. And the marriage of the sinker and the mine is supposed to last a year. Then, if the mine has not found its prey, the buffeting of the ocean is likely to cause a divorce and bring it harmlessly to the surface.

But they do not look harmless now, as one by one they go overboard. As soon as one row has come forward on its trolleys, there is a moment of climatic manipulation when the wires and the points of what they call " Clapham Junction " have to be changed over to enable the second series to be despatched. In and out of the men silently sweating over their job I find a way, until I come to the trolley at the end of the line, right back in the bowels of the ship. Here are two ratings who, as the mines go forward overboard one by one, advance towards the stern, standing on the truck to keep the mines from running away too fast. Want a ride, buddy? I climb up by the side of them, and as I balance there precariously, I think : Well, I've been given some strange lifts in my time, but never before brought up the rear in a procession of mines.

Plonk, swish, a sigh. The last of our load has disappeared. The men have surged away below to have cocoa and turn in. My companion, the Torpedo Gunner, has taken off his gardening gloves and retired to the wardroom. For a moment I am alone in the hollow tunnel where, a few minutes before, mines and men were anonymously intermingled and merged together in the darkness.

I cannot help thinking, as you would have done, of the damage and destruction these mines may cause, the human lives they may bring to an abrupt and horrible end. And then suddenly, the black cavern is not empty any more. It is full of ghosts. The ghosts of your friends and mine, reminding me that they are ghosts, because of a war thrust upon us, a war not of our seeking, and at once, my mood of dismay and sadness changes to one of clearer thinking. Surely it comes to this . . . the more efficiently we lay our mines, the sooner the war will be over, the less loss of life there will be in the long run. That is the way that the men who do the job reason it out. Aren't they right?

Down below in the wardroom, I join the Torpedo Gunner and Alan, just relieved from the bridge. Come on, Mr. H., you must have another grapefruit, Alan says. We've got something to celebrate. Alan has just heard that he is to go off for a medical to be transferred to be a pilot in the Fleet Air Arm. The veteran looks up from his chair with a twinkle. I suppose you think you're more sure of your harp that way, he suggests.

Whereupon we all have another grapefruit at the prospect.

Chapter Four

S.O.S. FROM HELL'S CORNER
THE SECOND

I HAD just had a bath and gone to bed because I reckoned it might be some time before I had a bath again, a hot one, I mean, when there came suddenly up the street of the little West Scottish fishing port a series of shrill, sharp blasts from the funnel of one of the tugs at the quayside. I knew what that meant. A warning that the crew were wanted urgently on board.

It was midnight. I tumbled out of bed again, put on four jerseys and my sea boots, and five minutes later was stumbling down the street in the blackout. As I passed the door of the Town Hall, I heard snatches of music and snatches of farewells, as some of my companions on the voyage went back to duty, running past me, with a girl's voice still warming their mind : Come back soon, and we'll finish our dance.

All ocean-going tugs which can operate in the North Atlantic are at half an hour's notice, day and night, to sail again from the moment they put back into their base. It does not matter whether the last trip took two days or two weeks, if the men go ashore, they must never be farther than a few minutes' distance. And in our case, the time from when the signal came through that hundreds of miles away out at sea a certain ship had been torpedoed and was in distress, to the moment when our sturdy little 600-ton boat glided smoothly away from her moorings, was exactly twenty-eight minutes.

The captain, who in peacetime had been a Humber River pilot, was already in his duffle coat. Every one aboard ? I asked. We're only short of two " ginger beers," he replied. Ginger beers? I echoed. And then I realized that this was rhyming slang for the second and third engineers.

As he stood there counting his crew of twenty-seven coming back over the plank, deep-sea fishermen from Icelandic waters, side by side with militiamen like the Sparks who a year ago had been a school teacher in St. Helen's, he reminded me of a monk with his hood up over his head, watching novices pass from the world and its pleasures, back into a shut-away, solitary retreat. For all the time that we were out at sea, journeying a thousand miles in our quest, we never saw another ship of any sort until the very last day, when we were close to harbour again, not even the fellow-tug operating with us from another port in our search.

It was calm enough, the first two hours going out. A lovely night. A great expanse of stars, and my spirits soared, remembering the magnificent job our crew of " novices " had done on their previous trip, when at sea for ten days, they finally found the ship they were after and towed her in safely to port. Her crew had already been rescued. That 10,000-ton freighter now lives to carry cargo another day.

At half-past two, the first engineer, who had thrown up a most successful coal business in Blackpool to volunteer to go back to sea, came up on to the bridge for a breather, and suggested a cup of cocoa down below. I was delighted with the idea. Even when later he said in a warning voice : We'll be going round the corner in a minute, I did not realize what was coming, and went on drinking my cocoa. But I never finished the mug. The last thing I remember was it being jerked across the table on to the floor as we met the full weight of the gale, and not a second too soon I was fighting my way up the companionway, to find oblivion in the mate's cabin.

He never performed a nobler act in his life than giving up his bunk, snugly tucked away beneath the wheelhouse. A man of fifty, this First Officer had sailed before the mast as a youngster, had prospected for gold, had been a Company Sergeant-Major with the Australian forces in the last war, and like all men who have done tough jobs supremely well, he was gentle, kind, simple-hearted.

From now on, there was no rest, no abatement. In an official report I read these words. "Rescue work is probably the roughest of all sea service, but they carry on with a splendid determination." In the next cabin to mine, through the night Sparks, listening for signals and feeling as seasick as I always do, carried on, sticking at his job, ironically writing in the logbook what must have seemed something of an understatement to him. Here is one entry. "Vessel pitching and rolling heavily to sea and swell."

Every other moment, you could feel the tug almost lifted right out of the water and then it came down with such a tremendous smack square upon the waters that the rubbing band, just above the water-line, made a dull thud as though the ship were hitting some extremely alien object. Several members of the crew confided in me during the rest of the voyage, that on their first trip they had believed again and again that they had hit a mine.

But they take it all in the course of the day's work. On the last trip they had had a signal to look out for a Sunderland plane which would be assisting them in their search. At the hour of the rendezvous a plane came over the horizon and approached nearer and nearer, but they did not worry, they went on ploughing ahead. And then suddenly when it was two hundred yards from their stern, they saw the black crosses on its underwings ; it was a four-engined reconnaissance plane of the enemy, and before they could get at their gun, the bombs had fallen. They were saved by the coolness of their captain. Just as though he was taking a ship down the river in peacetime, he stood up in monkey's island above the wheelhouse, and at the last split second, shouted Hard over to starboard, and round she came in the nick of time and the bombs fell harmlessly twenty feet away in the water.

Now the Mull of Kintyre is far behind us and Inistrahull lighthouse and Tory Isle and Bloody Foreland and the soft blue hills of Donegal, and there is nothing on the horizon except the great grey sea sweeping towards us, battering at us. In vain. These tugs are immensely sea-worthy. A great tribute to the design of a British company who, when war came, immediately gave their services for the benefit of the nation.

I was up on the bridge just before twilight the next evening, hanging on to the rail and straining my eyes for the sight of anything, anything. This is the hour when the U-boats surface and having stalked their prey all day, strike. This was the hour when, a few days before, a Dutch tug whom I had visited at the quayside while I was waiting to go to sea, had seen what they mistook at first sight for a periscope on the horizon.

It turned out to be something very different. A man standing up on a raft, desperately seeking to attract attention, while his six fellow Danes, who had been hopelessly adrift for three days, hung on to his legs, trying to keep the warmth of hope flowing through their own limbs. They were rescued an hour later . . . and do you know, the only common language in which they could thank and converse with their rescuers, was the language of the Huns who had sunk them. There's irony for you !

At this hour, I suppose in London, a voice said at my side, all the office folk will be queueing up for their buses to get home, greedy for another hour of daylight so that they can reach the safety of their homes before the black-out and, maybe, the sirens come upon them. And here we are, praying for the darkness to settle down an hour earlier. It's a topsy-turvy business, isn't it ?

It was the chief engineer, and the feeling in his voice was because on one of their trips our tug had gone out to rescue a ship on which he knew the second engineer was his greatest friend. You can imagine what his feelings were when they reached the spot as far as they could reckon and steamed round and round and found no trace. No trace at all, except a lifeboat floating past them, unnamed, and its only content an empty aspirin bottle. And you can imagine, too, what his feelings were when he reached port again and heard the great tidings that his friend had been saved by another ship.

He went on : "Do you know how to be a weather prophet?" I shook my head. "Well, I'll give you a couple of tips. At the hour of the sun going down, if the wind freshens a little but not too much and there is a slow rising glass, that means the night ought to be fairly quiet. And then he added something, as our conversation was temporarily interrupted by a great fountain of sea breaking over us ; I always say that when you go to sea, you can divide ships up into two classes. Whether you look up at the seas or down at them. There was no doubt which we were doing !"

No doubt at all. And later that night, in the middle watch, unable to sleep, I was very grateful when the first mate came in to his own cabin in search of some cigarettes, but I reckon that was only his excuse to have a yarn and thus make the early hours of the morning pass more swiftly for me.

As he stood astride the cabin, somehow keeping his balance, you would have seen behind him on the wall the framed snapshot of a pretty woman leaning over a rustic gate against a background which seemed overwhelmingly rural at that moment. His wife. As though he could guess what was in my mind, he volunteered : "You know, I often think it's much worse for those who wait at home and wonder how we are getting on. But I tell her she's luckier now than if she had been married to me in the early days of the century.

"It was in 1902," he went on, "when I left Liverpool on the *Lurlei*, bound for Iquique, and we were over eleven months at sea, and seventy-eight days off the Horn we were battling and after six weeks—six weeks, mind you, not six days—we found ourselves back in exactly the same spot. You've seen how we all hate the twilight on board, but I don't think it is as bad, myself, as those days when that was the time we had to go aloft and strain and sweat to change sail, often enough, and the blood poured down our arms from our nails, until I've seen men slip and lose their hold and be washed astern. Lost.

"Yes, eleven months it took, that voyage. And finally, when we were close to the Falkland Isles, we met a dead calm, and a tug came out and offered to take us in but the captain sent him away. We had only half a pint of water a day, mind you, we were chewing bone studs to quench our thirst and we shouted out to the tug how thirsty we were, and I can remember the captain swearing at us—he went mad afterwards—and shouting back : You'll be thirstier to-morrow. . . .

"You see, he would not stump up the two hundred quid the tug wanted. And the very next day, a favourable wind came and filled our sails and into the harbour we went and the men mutinied and refused to go out to sea again, and they were put to work by the prison authorities fixing the telegraph poles across the island. Those same telegraph poles which they say, at the beginning of the last war, picked up the news of the German fleet's presence in the vicinity and led to our first sea victory."

As though to point the contrast between those days and now, behind him on the wall swung a lamp, backwards and forwards, like the pendulum of time ; the same kind of lamp which must have lighted the last sailing ship on which he sailed, "the perfect *G. T. North*, the loveliest barque that ever left our port," as Masefield called it, the same lamp now fixed in our cabin, as a secondary light in case one of those dull, heavy thuds turned out to be a mine after all and the electric light fused.

The next morning I had my first meal, a couple of dry biscuits, and the next morning after that I became more optimistic and had some tinned grapefruit—very tasty. And they ragged me about the way I was diminishing their emergency rations, especially two boys who knew a thing about it, because they had been on the *Altmark*, transferred from the *Graf Spee*, where the food had been fine, they said —strawberries and cream for their tea. But on the *Altmark* their job had been to ladle out the midday meal, a ladleful of potato soup ; day after day.

And they are still smiling, though they have both been torpedoed again since in other ships, and still they play their mouth-organs on the tug at night, while the firemen down below played pontoon, though no one, I discovered, had yet thought of the idea of having a sweepstake on the length of each trip.

Another day and still the search went on ; another dusk and I am up in the chart room, opening out of the wheel-house, looking at the map with the captain—we call this Hell's Corner the Second, he said with his finger drawing a line from the north-west corner of Ireland far out into the Atlantic—when in came Sparks with the signal he had just received from our shore station, in answer to one we had sent out twelve hours before. " Go on searching till dusk and then if no sign of ship, return to harbour."

Sparks was grinning, because it meant that with any luck, the ship would get back on Saturday night in time for the Wrens' party. But the captain was not grinning. There's another hour yet, he said, meaning Don't think of turning round yet, and in the same breath, added gruffly : Who put the covers on the machine-guns ? Take them off again.

The accursed hour. Every dusk for these men at sea. And that particular hour seemed like the longest of the voyage to me, because all the time I could not help thinking about the ship we were searching for and wishing that we could have had the same luck as our crew had had on its previous voyage.

But that is the luck of the draw. They take it as it comes, and when we got back to the smooth waters of the harbour again, it was to find that a signal awaited them, a signal of encouragement ; to congratulate them on what they had done a week before. " *Your ship did very good work in bringing back the ' Fishpool ' in very difficult weather conditions.*"

Alongside us was the other tug, which had been employed on the same search. In the dusk I stepped across from our decks to theirs and silhouetted against the darkening sky was a great raft, all that they had found. For a moment, sadness possessed me, and then I saw beyond its silhouette, the thin, fresh buoyant crescent of the new moon, symbol of new hope, and before I turned the corner of the quayside back into the world, instinctively I found myself bowing nine times and wishing, for the men with whom I had sailed, good hunting and good fortune in the long months to come.

Chapter Five

THE CAPTAIN WORE FLANNELS ON THE BRIDGE

You SEE, there's nothing that the Navy can't do. It was not a boast. It was not a personal expression of opinion. It was simply intended for a statement of fact about which there was no argument. You would have felt the same had you been there in my place, perched on a wooden ledge in the lee of the Transmission Station for shelter from a half gale of wind and rain on board one of our Hunt class of destroyers out on a North Sea patrol.

We had left port early that afternoon, it was now close on the middle watch and my companion, who had just spoken, was the gunner's mate. And he was to be married the next Sunday in the village church of Higham in Kent. He had been courting for four years—and I gathered that the way of true love had not run altogether smoothly—but he was not referring to that in his statement about the Navy's omnipotence. Instead, we were discussing a sortie in which he had been engaged earlier in the year when a landing party from his previous ship had helped blow up some bridges in Boulogne. On that occasion, the gunner's mate had found himself a platoon commander. Which had caused me to ask whether it had not felt strange to go into action *off* his ship. That in its turn had prompted the answer—There's nothing that the Navy can't do.

Although I have done so many trips with the Navy since the war that I have long since ceased to feel any surprise at the miraculous efficiency of the Service, all the same, every time I go to sea again, however rough the swell, however dark the night, I never fail to register once again with gratitude and relief, above the creaking and groaning of the ship alive to a thousand sounds, a note recurring again and again of quiet and unassailable optimism.

My destroyer had done a particularly fine job only the other day, when she had gone within a few thousand yards of enemy occupied territory and pumped shells into the harbour and invasions preparations, and had the satisfaction of seeing great fires running up the breakwater, as light as day. And gone back the next night, when the cover and element of surprise had vanished, and done the whole job once again, having the satisfaction this time of seeing a torpedo from an E-boat miss her stern by a yard; but most of all, the satisfaction of seeing that E-boat, a moment later, lifted right out of the water by the effect of a full calibre shoot.

The gunnery officer had taught me that phrase. He had said : The gunner's mate is as tickled about his marriage as though he had just brought off a full calibre shoot. The gunnery officer, on these patrols, spends most of his nights in the coldest part of the ship, perched in a simian attitude on the superstructure which is higher even than the bridge, in the Director. As he had been, in peacetime engaged in a woollen manufacturing business in Ireland, I asked him his recipe for keeping warm. He had to confess that he wore thick, pink woollen combinations. Why pink? Because he's a communist, shouted in chorus the rest of the wardroom. Apparently, he had been heard on one occasion to suggest that the Irish rather than the English, were the chosen people of the world.

Fighting my way in the wind, I left the shelter of the T.S. and slid up the companion ladder to the bridge. They were just changing over ; the middle watch was about to commence. So far, a quiet night, from one point of view. Not that the trip already had been without its excitements. Soon after leaving port, there had been an air battle directly overhead. The sudden fingers of smoke in the ice-blue November sky seemed so remote from the speed of the changing pattern above our craning necks. And then the reality. . . .

Like a thunderbolt from Jove, the heavens opened and through the clouds came hurtling almost at our bows, a German fighter, rocketing to its doom. Did it really happen ? For the sea had in a single instant of time swallowed up its dead. But there was still a sign left. Floating soddenly on the water, the parachute of the pilot who had tried to bale out too late. Too late.

If you had felt any pity, you would have found it swallowed up by a different emotion, when a few miles farther on we passed a lightship which signalled to us that it had been bombed and machine-gunned that afternoon. Are you all right ? we asked. Their inherent cheerfulness comes across the water in their reply. Yes, thank you, our own supply ship is on its way out to us. When you have spent several days on board one of these little toy red bobbing ships, you feel a personal affection for them[1] and I found myself thinking as we steamed on our way. . . . I wonder if they are still eating onions for their tea, their favourite method of varying the monotony of their food.

I am beginning to feel more and more thankful that I held back from the savoury at dinner of bacon and cooked cheese. Later in the night the gunnery officer was sorry that he had not. And ate mine up into the bargain ! I put that on record without malice, but with some satisfaction nevertheless.

Fortunately, the doctor offers me the bunk in the sick bay. The only free bunk in the ship. Very decent of him, and I am thankful to go below for a bit. In every passage,

[1] See Godfrey Winn's *On going to the Wars*, page 99.

round the head of every companionway, we stumble over sleeping bodies. Some of them doubtless will be my friends from number six mess, which I visited earlier in the evening. That's where one of the two ship's mascots lives. There's a fox's brush nailed to the top of the masthead. And there's also a kitten called " Soot," whom the boys are trying to coax now to sleep in a tiny, beautifully made miniature hammock swung close to the deck in number six mess.

It was in this mess that I met a solicitor serving as an A.B., who used to work in Lincoln's Inn in peacetime, but already the metamorphosis was so complete that he might have been born a son of Popeye. In one corner here, two boys were intent over a board, a new version of the game " Attaque " in which the cardboard piece marked Admiral took everything. Away in the distance, a gramophone was playing the " Song of the Volga Boatman."

But now all is quiet, even the mouth-organist, who earlier was encouraging his mates of No. 1 gun crew, huddled round the Mounting aft. In ten seconds, I've got my sea boots off ; in five minutes I am asleep, despite the distraction of the galaxy of lovely ladies, which the doctor has pinned up on the wall, though I should have thought they would have tended rather to send up than down the temperature of his patients !

The next thing I remember is being woken by the bell that resounds through every compartment of the ship, and has one meaning only ; it summons every one to Action Stations. The ship is rolling worse than ever, but somehow, I get into my seaboots again, and am out of the security of the sick bay into the darkness of the sliding decks, and immediately the blackout hits me like a wall. There is no hope of a guide now. I've got to get back on to the bridge, and it is extraordinary when you have got to do something on your own, how in the end you do find a way.

I arrived to hear the captain, who was awarded the D.S.C. for his work in Norway, giving the command in his quiet, unruffled voice : Challenge her again. At his side the first lieutenant wishes me a polite good-morning. I may say, it is still a very dirty night.

Across the darkness there stands out in startling relief, the scarlet port lights of a ship. Already challenged, it has not answered. In any case in that position off the coast it should strictly not be showing any lights at all. On the bridge in every one's consciousness is the thought growing every second that it may well be a German raider, and behind us in the Director, the gunnery officer is concentrating on getting his range.

There is a pause which seems to lengthen like the road to the horizon, and in it I remember several things. How, when the captain at church parade read the bans of the coming marriage of the gunner's mate, he afterwards gave out the hymn—"O God Our Help in Ages Past"—and the ship's company who had presented the prospective groom with a silver cruet, insist that some connection was intended.

I also remember that I took off my lifebelt, the simplified form of life jacket you now wear at sea, and left it in the sick bay. Very stupid of me. And then apropos the challenged mystery ship, there comes into my mind the story they told me in the wardroom of the member of their crew, who when our destroyer was alongside a sister ship, was being filled up with some tall yarn over the side, but had his retort ready all right. Pointing up at the masthead, he exclaimed : " See that, chum ? Well, we've been foxed already once in this ship."

We were taking no chances to-night. Another second, and a shell would have crossed the bows of the reluctant trawler who at last answered our signal correctly, but still gave no explanation of why she was showing so much light. I wonder if she will ever know how close she was to destruction.

Every one relaxes. A moment later, the order is given Negative Active Stations. Regretfully the captain says to me : I am afraid it is too rough for E-boats to-night. Number One, who was mentioned in despatches at Dunkirk, offers me a black bullet, that is a bull's eye, out of a tin sent to him from a friend in Northumberland, whom he assures me lives in a village where no siren has yet sounded. And never will, he adds, because in the event of an air raid, it is the village policeman's job to go down the street banging a gong, but not one of the villagers would be brave enough to waken him when he is asleep.

I go below again. It is nearly five o'clock and I am glad of another couple of hours " kip," but when I return to the bridge the captain is still there. He has not left his bridge since three o'clock yesterday afternoon, and sometimes surely in the long night watches, he must see in his mind's eye, as he peers into the fog and rain and storm, a different scene, the peace of the blue Shropshire hills, which is his home ; and sometimes, too, I wonder if he murmurs under his breath the familiar words :

> " In summer time on Bredon,
> The bells they sound so clear ;
> Round both the shires they ring them,
> In steeples far and near,
> A happy noise to hear."

But the only bells that he will hear at sea are the three sharp, shrill ones which summoned me from my bunk.

In peacetime, the captain plays cricket for the Navy, and his method of keeping warm is to wear a pair of white flannel trousers, and over that a pair of black corduroys, and over his head a monk's hood. Occasionally during the night, he would slump for a quarter of an hour into a blue chair which might have come straight from the parlour of a seaside boarding house. It seemed so incongruous in a way, stuck there on the bridge, and yet its presence there was so typical of life in a destroyer, life which no less disciplined is always so much less conventional than in any other class of ship in the Royal Navy proper.

A great convoy passes as we come in again from patrol, there must have been a hundred ships. It would have given

Haw-Haw a pain in the neck, but it gladdens the one hundred and fifty hearts of the ship's company to see it. And down below in the wardroom, we celebrate the advent of leave—the ship is going into dock for minor repairs—and our return to port by having a " Horse's Neck."

The chief stoker, " No Legs," as they call him affectionately on the ship, has already told me that to-morrow he will be off to his beloved Norwich. And the chief engineer volunteers suddenly that he has been married for twenty-seven years, and he thinks it is a good thing to be wed to a sailor, because when your wife sees you on leave, it is always a pleasant surprise and never a habit. I wonder if the gunner's mate has found that out by now. . . .

But to return to the voyage now almost over. An A.B. knocks on the door of the wardroom with a list of the gramophone records bought out of the canteen profits. I notice there is a selection from the *Mikado*, several Bing Crosbys, " The Sailor with the Navy Blue Eyes," and what's this I see neatly copied out half-way down the page ? " The Song of the Vulgar Boatman."

I have to point this out to the gunnery officer who says it reminds him of a signal famous in Naval history. On one occasion, the flagship of the Mediterranean fleet, arriving at Gibraltar, could not wait a second to anchor before sending off a signal to shore. " *Send the Admiral's woman on board at once.*"

However, half an hour later, another signal followed. " Between ' Admiral ' and ' woman,' read ' washer.' "

We all go off to wash and clean ourselves up for the shore. Another voyage is over and the next time I go to sea in a destroyer, the winter is over, too, a heat wave is blistering the camouflaged paint, and sailing with yet another convoy, I discover to my delight that the English Channel belongs again to us. But turn over the page . . .

Chapter Six

THE ENGLISH CHANNEL STILL BELONGS TO US

THE seaside town was so familiar, I had been there for one of its famous firework displays the year before the war, but now I felt like a ghost walking down the promenade and hearing my footsteps echoing behind me in the silence of the June morning. It was as silent as Pompeii and I was the only sightseer. Where were the throngs of yesterday? Where were the winkle sellers? The ice cream merchants? The hot and sticky children for whom once upon a time this London by the sea was an excursion paradise?

The grand hotel on the front was still open, but now its only patrons seemed to be the families of men in Naval uniform. A little band of them bore down on me as I was having my solitary lunch. Is it true you're coming aboard with us on this trip? one said. Mutual recognition followed and that pleasant exchange of courtesies which is always the prelude to a trip at sea, for the Navy are the best hosts in the world.

An hour later, the loneliness of that deserted promenade was forgotten, the cold feeling of another plunge into the unknown quite forgotten, as I stood on the bridge of their ship and my eye caught sight of the miniature figure of a sailor, pinned upright on the rail, so polished that it glittered like silver in the sun. We put great faith in our mascot, they assured me.

At the same time I noticed that instinctively they glanced upwards in the heat haze at Bella, their pet balloon, which apparently had more than earned her keep on many recent occasions. For this was the twenty-sixth consecutive trip that this destroyer had done, guarding the convoys that pass and repass the Dover Straits and always get through despite the shelling and the dive-bombing.

What followed was a treat for me ; routine for them ; we set out in brilliant daylight—can this be war ?—but every one is immediately tense, knowing how deceptive the blue, calm waters can be. The first signal was sent forth. The guest is curious and excited. What was it ? I asked the captain. He grunts : I've just told the ship in front that I don't like her red behind. And what's her reply ? His face relaxed. She says that she likes it herself because it means that she will soon have to go on boiler leave for repainting.

Our destroyer is due for boiler leave, too. They talk of it, as of an oasis in the desert, down in the wardroom when we have our last meal of the day, with no alcohol. No Dutch courage, as Number One puts it.

Perhaps he is remembering their last trip when an enemy aircraft suddenly circled a convoy and dropped a stick of heavy bombs astern. One bomb made a direct hit on a ship in the convoy, causing a huge sheet of flame. Immediately the guns at Griz Nez opened fire and a salvo of four shells straddled the convoy, the nearest landing only forty feet away from our destroyer. Another bomb missed our destroyer so nearly that it took both the dynamos and the steering gear off the board.

You can imagine that a great number of other things happened after that. But in the official report, the captain wrote this sentence as his summing up : "*At daylight a fighter escort arrived and had a heartening effect on the men after a rather tiresome night.*" What do you think of that for understatement ?

But the dawn is still a long way off. No one will leave the bridge again for nearly twenty-four hours, and every member of the crew will stay at Action Stations through the night and most of the next day. When I came to the group huddled round Number One gun, a voice out of the darkness greets me : "The last time I saw you was at The Anchor, at Shepperton." That peaceful riverside pub, with the graceful church on one side of the square and the whole scene, with the lilac trees in bloom above the dark red brick wall and the glint of the river curving away into the distance, so reminiscent of a musical comedy backcloth. What a long way off it seems now.

A few minutes later, I am knocking on a little steel door which leads into a dome at the back of the bridge, rather like an outsize in rear gun turrets. This is the Director. Here the Gunnery Officer squats with his picked crew of three on guard until we reach port again, with instant telephone communication to every corner of the ship.

Come inside, too, if you can make it. It's a deuce of a squeeze, isn't it? For a moment you have the impression that you are in a box at the opera. The auditorium is in darkness, the curtain is about to go up. The Gunnery Officer says: "Actually a night when nothing happens is almost more exhausting than when we get shot up, because the sense of tension remains and there is no action to compensate."

The Gunnery Officer in peacetime was a great gardener. He has recently bought himself an estate in a village called Down Thomas in Devonshire. When will he see it again? He pushes the memory away from his mind on active service, he produces his thermos and suggests that I have some Oxo. We used to have cocoa, he adds, but we can't afford the sugar now.

After having been jammed there only half an hour, I crawled out of the dome again, already so stiff that it was good to be able to stretch my legs on the bridge. Midnight. You sense the tension so much that you almost tiptoe across to the rails. We are now approaching a channel which they have nicknamed "Bomb Lane," as opposed to "Shell Alley." The only positive sound is the tick-tock, tick-tock of the log, like the beat of eternity, or is it the beat of your own heart?

Sometimes a buoy, when we pass by, starts to ring its knell, so sweet and melancholy, so like church bells on a Sunday evening. Our captain, who is twenty-six and about to take the plunge into matrimony on his next leave, in Winchester Cathedral, murmurs almost under his breath:

" They always remind me of our chapel bell at school on a Sunday night. I used to hate it because it meant the end of a week-end and I knew that I had not done my prep." And now we don't have a week-end, he might have added. Sunday is just the same as any other day to us.

To digress for a moment, that reminds me of a visit I paid not long ago to the Liverpool docks. For three days I tramped many miles and jumped into the holds of many ships being unloaded by the Merseyside dockers, the majority of whom are doing a magnificent, front-line job to-day, but it must also be put on record that there are still some laggards who do not seem to realize that it does not matter what wages they earn or how much they get paid for over-time or working on Sundays, if at the end of it all we do not win the war.

What would happen to them then ? What would be the final fate of those—and you find them on every front still —who unable to see further than their own wage packet, persist in throwing a spanner into the works ? It is only too obvious what would happen to them. If Hitler came to Liverpool, they would be turned into chain gangs and receive no wages at all, but only the whip lashes of their conquerors.

Those who go to sea are more realistic or more altruistic ; it depends on your point of view. But you would soon become conscious yourself, if you spent much time among them as I do, that the only coins which have any value in their eyes, are those of comradeship, efficiency and guts.

My last evening at Liverpool I had the pleasure of being the guest of the Navy—on shore for once, when I visited the Flotilla Club which has lately been opened on the quayside for the destroyer and corvette crews. Here the men can slip ashore for an hour and be happy. They have not got to put on their Number Ones, they come in their overalls and their dungarees and have a glass of beer, and on the impromptu stage, one turn follows another.

As we enter, two Dutch seamen are singing the songs

of their own country and they are followed by a group of Poles, and finally a British gunlayer's mate who is sailing at dawn, obliged with " Way Down Upon the Swanee River," and to us it is as though the voice of Paul Robeson were piercing the haze of tobacco smoke and good cheer.

Afterwards, we all linked hands and sang "Auld Lang Syne." And they wished me luck on my own next voyage, and we reminisced about their own last one, when by one of those strange coincidences which are a commonplace of war, my corvette passed their destroyer coming into port. And their destroyer had quite a gash in her side, now repaired, from a rescue party in an Atlantic storm, which is portrayed in paint in the picture reproduced in photo-grauve in this book. A picture painted by their Number One, Peter Scott, who in peacetime was in a class by himself in the depicting of wild birds on the wing.

His ship and its crew have had many stirring adventures in the last year, but now as the boys gathered round me and we had one final drink, all they seemed concerned about was my future. " Now take care of yourself and see that next time you don't have to walk back through The Drink," they exclaimed in chorus. But ne'er a word about themselves, their own future prospects, their rigid disciplined time-table. They don't get paid overtime because of an attack or twice their wages because they are due to sail at dawn on a Sunday morning. They just take it as it comes and this is their farewell party in the Flotilla Club. Too soon the night swallows them up, they go back to their ships and all is silence once more on the waterfront.

All is silence still on the bridge of our destroyer going down the Channel in the warm darkness of a summer night. Every now and again the Navigation Officer is asked to take our bearings. Whereupon he disappears like an old-fashioned photographer, under a curtain beside the bridge, and by the light of a flash-lamp looks at his charts. The precision of the whole voyage is miraculous. At the conference before the convoy set off, the commodore told

This photograph is a reproduction of a painting by Lieut. Peter Scott, of a rescue scene in which his destroyer took part.

the captains at exactly what moment they would be expected to pass every buoy during the night. We are up to our schedule to a second.

Suddenly there is a flash away to the left. You see, we've reached " Shell Alley " at last. Is it flak or is it a shell ? If you are in Dover, you count eighty and then you know. Someone has a stop-watch handy. We all duck at fifty, I am told cheerfully. One thing I like about the Navy so much is that they never put up any false façades.

As we waited for our fate, I remembered a story about General Freyburg who was once discussing with a friend the problem of fear, and the general confessed that he had found a perfect remedy for the hiatus when a man is waiting to see if a shell is going to hit him or not. I take bets with myself, he explained, as to whether the shell is going to score a direct hit or not, and I get so interested in seeing who is going to win that I forget to feel frightened.

Fifty. Duck, man.

I put my head down below the rails and a tin hat I've borrowed rolls off, making a din on the deck like the trump of doom in the immensity of the silence. A second later we all take a deep breath and come up again. Now to the left in the neighbourhood of Boulogne, the whole sky is aflame with flak and explosions which must be our bombers going over on a great attack on the invasion ports. It heartens us to see the trails of their progress, but how slowly the time passes. . . .

The captain himself is crouching on a three-legged stool ; it is exactly like the stool on which Cinderella always sits in the kitchen scene, when she is left sadly behind and her sisters go to the ball. Our captain keeps on having a hunch that he can see a dim, alien object in the distance, an E-boat maybe . . . but in the end it always turns out to be another of our escort vessels !

At the dawn, a single Blenheim comes off the coast to help guard us, making our own solitariness seem somehow more profound, and I found myself remembering what the commodore had said to me before setting out. He said :

" When the dawn comes, I never cease to be surprised to find the Channel in front of us so empty. In peacetime, I was so used to dawn in the English Channel in June and the whole sea crowded with shipping, coming from all corners of the world. Now there is nothing except us."

As the sun mounts serenely to presage another blazing day, our spirits mount too, and Number One gun crew start lessening the strain of their continuous stand-to by playing a portable gramophone. A jam session of records by Nat Gonella, and as though they can hear the music, the fighter escort which have come off the coast now to join the Blenheim, perform fantastic variations of their own mercurial dance. Or perhaps it is that they want to impress the group captain we have on board, and the squadron leader who wears the D.F.C. with bar on his tunic. They are doing the trip as I am, to see how the show really works ; so that they can go back to their Station and pass on the fruit of their knowledge for co-operation. Incidentally, in the next section of this book, in the very first chapter, you will see a reference to this same group captain. But there he is wearing white overalls and has just landed from doing a daylight sweep over France. . . .

Now we are passing Beachy Head ; it is a fine tonic ; it gives you a sense of freedom to glimpse those white cliffs again from the sea, and Number One and I discover that we were at the same prep. school, St. Christopher's, at Eastbourne, years ago. Just one more of the unexpected links which are always cropping up to give life a pattern.

Now, too, you can recognize faces again, after the long tense night. On the bridge, three sailors are standing waiting orders as runners. One I last saw playing a part in *Bitter Sweet*, the second was an announcer on the Australian radio, who has travelled a long way to do what he feels is his duty ; the third is the son of the most famous woman revue star our country has produced in the last decade. But already they have been swallowed up in the tradition of the Service. They look as though they have been standing to attention all their life.

Not until half an hour before we come into port does any one start to relax. Then the captain leaves his bridge to go down into his cabin to shave and change. That is also part of the Tradition, to go into port, looking as spick and span as though you had been out on holiday manœuvres. In his cabin while I am sharing his jug of hot water, my eye catches on his desk a framed quotation from something that Oliver Cromwell wrote in 1642. Perhaps you would like to have it for your desk too. " WELL, YOUR DANGER IS AS YOU HAVE SEEN, AND TRULY I AM SORRY IT IS SO GREAT. BUT I WOULD HAVE IT CAUSE NO DESPONDENCY, AS TRULY I THINK IT WILL NOT, AS WE ARE ENGLISHMEN."

We are just coming into harbour and through the loud speakers suddenly the ship is ablaze with music. And now they are playing the gramophone record which is the signature tune of our ship and has for every member of the crew a particular significance. " D'ye Ken John Peel ? "

I'll leave you to work out the connection—it's quite simple really, much simpler than a crossword puzzle, any-way—and go on to tell you that before I left the ship myself, all the officers took me aside in turn and said in an apologetic undertone : " I'm sorry we could provide no major excitements for you this time." To which I replied that I had enjoyed my sun-bathing trip very much, but I had been surprised it had been so quiet. Because, you see, I added, this was my thirteenth trip at sea since the war began.

Instantly the captain touched the little polished sailor attached to the rail of the bridge. Thank goodness you did not tell us that earlier, or we would never have had you on board, he said.

Chapter Seven

DRAKE ROLLED HIS DRUM AGAIN

I'M afraid you won't get any cocktails on board here, the steward said apologetically, as he helped me over the side with my bag. It was seven o'clock in the morning, and I had never felt less like cocktails in my life. Besides, I was only prepared for fireworks.

Later, he explained his greeting. He had been a cocktail shaker at the R.A.C. club in London's Pall Mall, and now by one of those contrasts which is a commonplace of war, he had become the steward on an ocean-going tug. He does not complain of the change. Secretly, he must feel mighty proud that he has been able to take it, especially after the feat which H.M.T. *Freebooter* (with the skull and crossbones as its distinguishing mark painted upon its bridge) performed during the trip that I was on board. Freebooter . . . that's a name to make the ghostly drum of Drake roll again, I thought, as we put out to sea, and I admit I couldn't help feeling rather happy, too, because I had been chosen to be the only writer on board to chronicle the voyage.

Mind you, at the time, it seemed a mixed privilege. Every one in authority imagined that we were in for a hot time. Actually it turned out to be a pleasure cruise— they taught me poker on board and how—and yet what would have happened if, say, a year ago, from under the very nose of the enemy, we had decided to move a giant floating dock of a displacement of twenty thousand tons, and to tow it hundreds of miles at an average speed of three and a half knots. Would we have got away with it unscathed ? Would we ?

But we did get away with it. And we set sail as Drake did, in broad daylight, and this last chapter in the naval section of this book is the story of that voyage which will go down in the history of the war as an epic achievement, and I promise you, I do not use the expression lightly. Indeed, I shall always be grateful that I was there myself, because it gives me a second chance in this book to pay a tribute to the men who still do not receive a sufficient meed of praise, the men who command and the men who serve in the vast flotillas of little ships which in peacetime the passengers on great luxury liners lightly dismiss as, for example, " fussy little tugs."

Fussy little tugs, indeed, exclaimed Captain B, the tug-master in charge of the three tugs, of which mine was in the centre, now sailing out of harbour with an escort which was worthy of Royalty. Three destroyers, two of them flying the Polish flag, a posse of M.L.'s, and an Ack-Ack ship with a solid and reassuring silhouette of massed guns, while overhead a multitude of aircraft gave us almost embarrassing support.

Captain B. craned his neck for a second. " Now I take my hat off to them every time I see them," he said. " Not that you'd ever get me up in one of them. Now a ship's different. I always say that I'm too wooden to sink, but I'm heavy enough to fall from one of them. I'd rather be a live coward any day, than a dead hero."

I said nothing. I was thinking of the other trip I had done in one of these ocean-going tugs, far out into the Atlantic ; of all the trips that these rescue tugs have performed in the war, salvaging hundreds of thousands of tons of shipping. I was thinking of the German aircraft that the skipper of one of the other tugs in our tow had destroyed by holding everything, including his fire, until the last moment. I was thinking of the tug, suitably named *The Englishman*, which gallantly went down with all its crew, in the course of its duties.

Captain B., who is a Trinity House boy and went to sea when he was thirteen, hails from Hull. They should honour his name there, for the successful completion of this gigantic tow has a deep significance since it means that when peace comes again, British tugs have earned a right to challenge every other nation for the work that there will be then, in plenty.

So there was romance, too, in our trip, though no one would suggest that the floating dock itself was a thing of beauty, least of all, I imagine, its crew of sixty Naval ratings and fifty odd dockyard men. In the evenings, when she was silhouetted against the dying light, she seemed full of secrets, full of the ghosts of the ships which had at some time or other been repaired in her, great ships like the *Royal Sovereign*. While in the daytime, she kept on reminding you of the Tower Bridge.

Indeed, after a few days you began to have a daylight nightmare that you were being pursued by the Tower Bridge and could not get away. That was from the strain of appearing to be stationary in the water, so slowly were we moving, and all the time the constant expectation of enemy attack. As for the strain on the two ropes, it gives you some idea when I tell you our eighteen-inch manila rope, which cost four hundred pounds new and was a hundred and twenty fathoms long, stretched an extra nine feet in the first two days.

And we were lucky in the weather, too, though the one bad day when we were rolling like a barrel, the three tugs showed their mettle all right. When I emerged again myself and reached the bridge, Wally the mate, with that slow smile I came to like and respect, remarked : " She's coming along nicely with a bone in her teeth." It was his way of referring to the moderate foam at the dock's bows. Then to vary the monotony of his own gaze from the constant oppressive presence of that sitting target, his eyes would wander away to one of the destroyers still guarding us. He had a particular affection for her. Because on Friday, May 10th, 1940, he had been in Rotterdam Harbour and his own ship had been sunk and it was this same destroyer which had brought him safely back to England to fight another day. So more than ever in the war does the whirligig of time bring its own revenges.

Wally gave me his cabin one night when he had a double watch, but usually I slept on a seat in the ward-room. One morning I was woken by the three sharp bells shrilling through the ship, which I sometimes think I shall hear all the rest of my life in my dreams. I recommend that signal to head masters who want to get their boys out of the dormitory on time. However many false alarms you have, you still get up on deck, with your " Mae West " on, within a minute. Another morning, I was woken by the captain of the tug itself, who was co-operating with Captain B. He was leaning over me and exclaiming : " It's a grand day." He was smiling, he looked pink and fresh and rested, although he had been up all night.

What is it that makes a man stand out from the rest ? Some instinct told me that this captain was such a man, even before I discovered that on his tunic, he wore a white ribbon that is almost as rare as the V.C. The white ribbon which is the proof that he sailed with Shackleton in the *Endurance* in the great Antarctic Expedition of 1914.

One night on the bridge, he told me something of his adventures, of the time when he and his companions were marooned on Elephant Island for four and a half months, while Shackleton struggled back to get help. In their hearts, they never expected to see him again. They existed during those four and a half months almost completely in darkness. How did you stick it ? I asked, redundantly.

He said : " One of my companions had a penny cookery book which his wife had thrown into his bag at the last moment. That and a few pages of the *Encyclopædia Britannica* which we had kept for pipe spills, were our complete library. We took it in turns each night in the hut to read. We propped up an empty sardine tin, filled it with some blubber fat and used as a wick a piece of one of our shirts, which gave a dim light for about six inches, and then the librarian of the evening would start reading aloud, but he seldom got further than the first recipe. Because then the most violent discussions would break out as to what was the best meal in the world. This was our way to try and blot out from our minds the knowledge that the only meal we could hope to have to-morrow and to-morrow were limpets gathered with our bleeding hands at low tide off the rocks."

Listening in the darkness beside me on the bridge was Bunts, whose home is in Weybridge where his father is Mine Host of the Royal Oak. Any time you're passing, there's a glass of beer for you on the house, he assured me. Thank you, Bunts. I do not know what your working hours were supposed to be, but I never once went on the bridge, day or night, when you were not on duty.

Then there was the boy who came from the island where there is not a single pub. Eriskay, the smallest in the Outer Hebrides, only three miles long and two and a half miles wide, with six hundred inhabitants, but all the same it possesses a wonderful war record. Every able-bodied man on the island is now in the Merchant Navy. None of them ever thinks of going into the Army or the Air Force. The sea is their birthright.

Many of the rest of our forty-six crew were either Geordies from Newcastle or Aberdeen fishermen. One of the latter, whose used to make many trips to the Faroes in peacetime, and was now a stoker, volunteered to me one day with a grin : " Now this is what I call a gentleman's life." I wondered if Chiefie would have agreed with that dictum. For when we set sail, our chief engineer from South Shields was wearing a spotless pair of white overalls, but by the end of the voyage his overalls were black, so were his gloves, and his face, too, for it was impossible to keep clean on board. Sometimes I used to go down in the wardroom and find him pushing back some coffee to keep awake, and with such a weight in tow, he must keep awake, he had to guard his engines with such desperate care. I shall always remember the night when his face suddenly lit up and he exclaimed : " Wait a jiffy, Godfrey, I've got something to show you." When he returned from his cabin, he was holding carefully by the tips of his oily fingers,

The name of his ship is not on his cap, but his smile is typical of every man with whom I have sailed.

a large coloured enlargement of his attractive wife and their two pretty little girls.

Chiefie was too shy to say anything more. He just took out a packet of cigarettes and with the silver paper wrapping he fashioned a little cup like a champagne glass, and then he moistened the bottom and proceeded to flick it up at the ceiling with such accuracy that it stuck. There were dozens of those symbols on the wardroom ceiling. The symbol of their thoughts and their dreams. *When we get into port again.*

It was seven o'clock in the morning when, well ahead of schedule, we ourselves got into port again. Up on the bridge, Captain B. was staring at the eight " fussy little tugs " which had come out to take the dock to its new moorings. His face was expressionless, as he stretched his stiff back and eased his jersey, for he had not had his clothes off for a week. I expected him to show some emotion, elation at his success, relief at our escape, something. But all he said was : " Well, I think I'll go and have a cat's nap."

And then I realized that it was simply one more job to him. How can Hitler hope to defeat such men as these ?

Act Two

Chapter One

THE CIRCUS

THEY call it a circus. It gives sometimes two, even three performances a day, but it is unlike any circus you or I have ever been to in days of peace. The only link in common is the gargantuan din as the performance is about to begin. But instead of the hurdy-gurdy or the clamour of the machines that work the side-shows, this is a different sound, the sound that will be for ever after imprinted on the consciousness of any one who has stayed for any time at an R.A.F. Station. The roar of engines revving up, when a show is about to start.

Thirty-six Spitfires, just off on a daylight sweep over enemy territory. It is afternoon. The hour when you were just putting on the kettle, perhaps, for a cup of tea. By the time you had washed up the tea things, they were back again.

But let us go back earlier than that. An hour before the symphony of the engines seemed to sweep the horizons away to infinity, the three squadrons engaged in the circus were lounging about in their dispersal huts, waiting for orders. Two Home squadrons and one formed entirely of Canadian personnel.

In the Canadians' hut, some are reading papers from home. One fellow is methodically filing his nails. Another is half asleep on a bed against the wall where, over his head, there is a picture cut out from a magazine, of a luscious young lady, also reclining, but in a very different kind of costume from the pilot. The title under the picture is " Siesta." What a chance, what a contrast for an artist with imagination, I find myself thinking.

In another dispersal hut, that small, stereotyped,

insignificant-looking building, which one day will provide a setting for a play as great as *Journey's End*—will it be called *Journey's Beginning*?—a gramophone is playing. Last year when I visited this same station, it was " Martha "—" Martha " all day long. Now the rage is a tune called " Rhum Boogie," sung by a star as new as the faces around me, Carmen Miranda. In one corner, some members of the flight are having a round of whisky poker. It's a nice, cheap game, they said. We used to play bridge, one added, but we gave it up after a time, as we always seemed to be losing our fourth.

While in the third dispersal hut the highlight in decoration was a barrel, painted all over with rings of red, white and blue, with the word " Beer " inscribed just above the tap. But don't be deceived, it's only water. They drink a good deal between sweeps. In the air, one told me, you sweat as much in a Spitfire on Ops. as on a Rugger field.

Suddenly the telephone rings, not shrilly, but almost apologetically, and the leader of the squadron goes to answer it, and there is a moment of suspended animation in the hut, but even before he puts down the receiver again, every one is collecting their gear, and a moment later, they come bundling out of the hut into the afternoon sun, gladiators in a Wellsian world, in their orange " Mae Wests," with their parachute harness under their arms, moving clumsily like jockeys on their way to the weighing-in.

Across the field they come, in twos and threes, all crowding together into one dispersal hut, where the wing-commander who is leading this sweep—in the morning their group captain had done so himself, in a pair of white overalls over his tunic with the D.F.C. and the D.S.O. and the A.F.C. upon it—stands with his carved, modern-Viking profile against a map, and explains the route that the circus is going to take.

Quietly he repeats the heights at which the three squadrons will operate ; he names the Station where they will pick up the other squadrons, for this is to be a big show, the biggest yet the circus has put on : and finally, he speaks of the towns in the circus's tour, and one name sounds strange in that setting, for it conjures up instinctively such different memories. Memories of a famous golf club house and pine trees and a casino at whose high table thousands of pounds used to change hands almost as swiftly as to-day a Spitfire's cannons—firing eight rounds a second—never fail to perform their appointed task. Le Touquet. And all those silly faces in smirking poses reproduced in the society papers.

Will that world ever come back again, you wonder, as your eyes go round the group of these young men who loathe publicity, and whose faces are half-smiling, not self-consciously into a camera, but at a vision secret to themselves, as they listen to the time-table. One takes out a fountain pen, I notice, and on the back of his wrist, writes down the places and the times. His maps are jutting out of the top of his flying boots. In peacetime, he was apprenticed to be an analytical chemist in Liverpool.

The briefing is over. The hut is empty, will stay empty for an hour and twenty minutes. We are walking beside one of the pilots towards his machine. I see that he has written something in ink, too, on the back of his " Mae West." R.I.P. He tells me that this is his twenty-third sweep.

Fitters are putting the finishing touches to his kite. One boy has a tin of grease in his hand, like a housewife uses, and his rag is a bit of an old flowered dress. He is polishing the side of the hood, so that it will slip back easily in a split second if the pilot has to bale out. His conscientious movements can so easily mean a chance to fight another day.

It occurs to me he is the stooge who never gets praised except by the pilots themselves, who know. Now the fitter is wiping the hood itself and then with a last devoted movement, the small mirror, no larger than a shaving glass, in which the pilot watches that vast eternity of space behind him for a pinprick of quicksilver which means an enemy fighter is coming in on his tail.

As soon as the pilot climbs into his machine and adjusts the inter-com. pad over his mouth, he becomes as remote as a surgeon wearing a mask over his face in an operating theatre. A curtain of din, too, divides him now.

As for the machines themselves, you cannot sense their speed and implacability in the air, until they take off. And then, as you watch them taxi away and leap into that other world which henceforth will be their tilting ground, the clover at your feet, the farm horses plodding in a field only a mile away, the red bus with its inscription, " Selected tours in England, Scotland and Wales," slowly puffing round the perimeter, with ground staff on their way to their tea . . . how mundane they all seem suddenly beside the indescribable glitter of the elements shining upon the wings of the three squadrons, as the first circles the airfield so soon to be joined by the second and by the third . . . and away . . . and we have only just time to reach the Operations Room to hear the first messages coming through on the R.T., as the united mass of the sweep crosses the French coast.

That, I guess, gives you some idea of the pace. And I wish you had been with me and had a pair of earphones over your head, too, for that would have given you an even more vivid idea of how the battle progresses, as you hear emerging from the shapeless, rasping cacophony of atmospherics, a warm human voice exclaim, as clearly almost as though he were there beside you in the listening cabin : " Mama, must I keep on weaving ? . . . Are there nothing but Spits ? . . ."

And then another voice : " Open out, boys, open out. The sun is behind us, keep a good look-out behind," and at once you have a flash-back in your own mind to that tiny shaving mirror. " Okay." Punctuating the R.T. transmission at intervals, came always that same interval signal, " Okay."

" Aircraft dead above. Okay. I can see our *friends*, they are at eleven o'clock to you now. There are quite a lot diving down behind us." This time, there is no okay,

instead a sudden silence, and then a nightmarish wireless
screech lifting the top off your head, which may mean
nothing but all the same you're sweating pretty badly
yourself, until that first quiet deliberate voice starts again :
" We'll do a circuit, right round to port . . . we'll see if
we can get one of those b——s. . . . Okay.

" They're coming down on us. Keep together, boys.
We're right in the beehive now . . . any one would think
there was a war on. . . ." And once again, that screeching
blast that can so easily mean everything or nothing, and
once again your palms are sticky, and then as though to
reassure those of us who have to be left behind, comes that
symbol of imperturbability. . . . Okay . . . going back
now. . . . Okay.

It hardly seemed a minute later that the leader's voice
was saying : " Re-form over Deal . . . passing over Dover,
I'll waggle my wings." And for the first time, the little
group listening round me relaxed in their chairs and leant
back smiling. The next moment I had taken my earphones
off and was out in the courtyard, jumping into the car so
as to get back in time to see them land.

It's no use trying to count. In any case, they won't
come in as they went off in formations of fours, so it doesn't
mean a thing, I kept on reminding myself, that here and
there they are plopping out of the heavens in solitary glory.
But what's that one doing ? Even I could see it was landing
all cock-eyed. Gosh, it's going right into the hangar. No,
it isn't. It's stopped . . . now little ants are running
towards it.

Afterwards I heard that it had planted its feet politely
and neatly in a flowerbed of antirrhinums ten feet away
from the wall. The wounded pilot, with a good portion of
the tail of his Spitfire blasted off by cannon, had still
managed to bring his machine home. The new circus has
its own traditions.

Meanwhile, another machine has landed ten yards away
from me, standing on the other side of the field. As I

watched the pilot climb out, I remembered how someone had told me to sniff for the smell of cordite, which he swore for the rest of his life would be the most exciting smell in the world for him, and to listen as the machines taxi into stillness and immobility again for the sound, as of the pipes of Pan, for the sound of the wind whistling through their now open cannon caps, the proof that they have been engaged.

The intelligence officer is pouncing with his notebook on this particular pilot, the squadron leader who has led one section of the sweep. But he says regretfully : " We saw plenty of them, but they wouldn't come in and play. They just stayed in the sun, and only nibbled at us. Still, the other boys got a squirt, I believe."

It wasn't for me to open my mouth or I would have reminded him of the record they possess up to date, that not one single bomber that has been escorted, has been shot down by enemy fighters. What losses there have been have all come from flak. To remind him, too, that on the notice-board of the mess, simple figures state a simple truth. Already this particular station has destroyed five hundred and eighty-one Jerries, with three hundred and twenty-seven probables. (And that was only up to the end of June, 1941, mark you.)

Well, if he wanted comfort for not having had a squirt, it came from another quarter. A fox terrier made a dash from the dispersal hut and started leaping and nibbling at his " Mae West." His master's expression changed, the sharp ridges beneath his eyes seemed to smooth out as he muttered : Hello, Pete. Good boy, Pete. How was he to know that it was your Spitfire ? I asked inanely. Oh, I don't like to let him down. I always land at the same spot, he replied, and went on to tell me that Peter had been in the Air Force ever since he was six weeks old.

By the time we got back to the mess, we heard that not a single Spitfire had been lost that day, and so later that evening my hosts and the fellows from another station, who had provided the other wing of the circus that day, met on earth for a change in the pub which is recognized as a kind of half-way house between their two airfields.

A good party, and the moment I remember most vividly was when an old friend of mine, at closing time, raised his tankard and unconsciously added the perfect postscript to this story of a day in the life of a fighter circus : " It's good to think of all those Nazis—and he pronounced the word as Mr. Churchill does—going to bed by candle-light to-night in Cologne and shivering in their cellars."

And yet as he drank up, I shivered myself. In sympathy with those who now at long last are getting a taste of their own medicine ? That question is redundant. No, I shivered in that bar full of tobacco smoke and the heat of good cheer, from a sudden premonition. My companion seemed so confident. Too confident. I was suddenly afraid for him. To-morrow's circus . . . and to-morrow's . . . how could he survive them all ?

It had been my second visit to that particular fighter Station, whose circus activities I have described in this chapter and which are now far more brilliantly portrayed from the inside in another book called *Readiness at Dawn* by Blake, the pseudonym for a squadron leader in the Operations Room, in peace-time well known in the world of the theatre. But the great value of his book lies not in its over-dramatization, but in its understatement. Read it, if you can. I warn you, you will feel very sober at the end. As I was feeling that night in the pub, despite the half a dozen drinks I had put away. Sober because of my memories of the ghosts which thronged that pleasant parlour. The ghosts of the men with whom I had made friends a year before, and described in my previous war book in the chapter called " Portrait of a Miracle Man."

But what I did not quote in that portrait was an extract from a letter I had received a few days after we had first met in his mess, written by one of the " so few," whose ghosts were thronging the bar that evening. We corresponded regularly, until the sudden silence to which there is no answer, but I know that Jack would not mind my repeating now his private intimations of that immortality that lies around them in the skies.

He wrote : " I wonder how much you realize the amount of fear a fighter pilot has to suppress ? It's a hell of a lot, and by far the great majority of us realize we are suppressing it. That accounts very largely for the superficial hatred some of us have for the quota of newspaper praise we get. The fighter pilot is exceptionally honest with himself—one of his chief virtues. Regarded in the searchlight of C. of E. morals, he's otherwise a fairly bad type, but a bloody good friend. Pal is a better word, but a trifle less expressive through being hackneyed.

" And now about those Proms. I'd really love to come one evening and I think I can manage it in about five days' time, when a spot of leave falls due. I'd prefer some Delius and Elgar—is there to be a programme of them ? I remember a concert about four years ago, containing the Enigma Variations, and some of Delius's songs. . . ."

There you have the enigma, the violently contrasting facets which go to the making of the diamond-like façade of the fighter pilot's make-up. It is the same with them all : the same with my companion who drank to the Nazis shivering in their beds. The first time we lunched together in London he surprised me by asking me abruptly for a passage from a broadcast I had given way back in the locust years when we all lived in Cloud Cuckoo Land. " I listened to it with Max," he went on. " You said something about there being three things you believed in ? Have you a copy of it ? I'd like to read it over again." The three things were sincerity, faith, and a sense of humour. There was no need for me to look up the file of dusty manuscripts, because my companion already possessed all three of those qualities in abundance. The faith in his machine and in himself as a pilot, and above all, the cause for which he was prepared to make any sacrifice, the sincerity that at the end of last summer made him sacrifice a safe job at the Air Ministry to go back on Operations, although as a wing-commander who had led sortie after sortie and been in the first bombing raid on Berlin, he had every justification to sit back and be content to pool his experience in the newcomers' melting pot. And the sense of humour, which that night made him tell me a story about Fritz and Hans, who as they sit quaking in their own shelters, with the R.A.F. droning overhead, are nowadays supposed to comfort each other with this snatch of dialogue.

Fritz : Have you heard about the other evening when the Führer went over Britain in a bomber with Goering to see all the terrible damage that the Luftwaffe has done to London ?

Hans : No . . . what happened ?

Fritz : Well, they set off . . . and after flying for some hours, the Führer suddenly looked out and saw below great waves of flames coming up towards the machine, the whole city ablaze. He rubbed his hands in glee, and patted the Field Marshal on the shoulder and shouted in his ear : " Your boys, Hermann, have certainly made a mess of London. I shall give you another medal for this."

Hans : And what did Goering say ?

Fritz : He shook all the medals on his stomach with an angry heave, and bellowed back : " Don't be so silly, Adolf, we have only reached BREMEN."

But my companion that evening will never in his Hurricane escort bombers over Bremen or Cologne again. He was last seen baling out into the Drink. And since then silence. His name was Wing-Commander Gillan. All his friends knew him as Gillo. It was he who told me, as I have written earlier in this chapter, to sniff for the smell of cordite which, you may remember, he swore would be the most exciting smell in the world for him, for the rest of his life. For the rest of his life. He did not guess how few more days the hour-glass had to run for him. It was left to the stranger in their midst to have that premonition, and grow suddenly silent, and suspect that he was taking his last look at a friend, and look more closely for that. And my last memory of Gillo before we all poured out into the darkness—Time, Gentlemen, Time—was of a glowing, smiling face, ready and eager to take the wings of the morning again.

So perhaps, after all, they are the lucky ones. If he had fear he quenched it from an inexhaustible draught of courage, compounded of sincerity and faith, and at least I understand now what it really means " they whom the gods love die young." So that they shall not know the weariness of spirit, the disillusionment, the infinite ordinariness of later life. They go out in their glory, they leave a comet trail behind them in the sky ; they want no pity, because they have *lived*.

Chapter Two

THE CATALINA THAT WAS ON STRIKE

I AM writing this in an hotel bedroom at Newcastle. It is my headquarters for a few days, during a speaking tour in this region for the Ministry of Information. You drive through the blackout, to a town where you have never been before, like Sunderland, and you enter a strange hall, and stand up on a bare platform, feeling your loneliness acutely in that moment when you face the sea of anonymous faces, with whom you have so little time to make contact, to pass on the sum of your experiences in different front-lines, before once more the darkness outside swallows you up. Sometimes there are two thousand potential friends in the audience : sometimes two hundred ; but I tell myself over and over again, to combat the loneliness of one hotel bedroom after another, that even if only half a dozen members of the audience go away with a greater and more vivid understanding of what the conflict is really like on other fronts from their own, then all the exhaustion and the complications of these endless journeys in war-time are more than worthwhile. And always I have held the view that the spoken word has infinitely more power and meaning than the written saga, however stirring the story it has to tell.

To-night I was talking about what it is like to fly on operations with the R.A.F., as I have been privileged to do on several occasions, and to refresh my memory before I set out for Sunderland, I looked through past pages of my diary, until I finally came to the section which covers one of the most dramatic incidents of the war to date, of which even now the whole story has not yet been told. The sinking of the *Bismarck*. And it is because I feel that these entries in my war diary, written down at the time and on the spot, may be of some importance in dispersing the mists of history as far as ordinary citizens are concerned, that I have decided not to compress or change the form of this chapter of my diary at all but to reproduce in their entirety the pages which concern the Catalina seaplane which found the *Bismarck*. But you must imagine when you are reading them that you have gone back in Time to that morning when the pursuit of the *Bismarck* summarily pushed all other headlines off the page. Ready?

In a remote corner of the British Isles, a few hours ago, I climbed into an R.A.F. motor-boat at the side of a loch, glittering in the sudden summer sunshine so that the lush-green of the trees dotted here and there on the miniature islands, and the scarlet of the rhododendrons in full flame were reflected dazzlingly in the water. What a perfect day for a picnic, someone said.

I agreed, though my thoughts were far removed. As yours would have been. For in the centre of the peaceful waters, with the sheen of peace upon them, riding serenely at anchor was a seaplane with an arch of wings so wide that already it has been nicknamed " The Flying Plank."

This was the seaplane which has recently made history. The Catalina flying boat which successfully searched for and sighted the *Bismarck* after the German battleship had been lost in the mists of darkness and fog for eight hours, and undoubtedly, in consequence, was the means of bringing about her final destruction. And in doing a magnificent job was herself so very nearly destroyed. Indeed, you realize that as soon as you clamber on board and discover beneath the twin pilots' seats the large fresh yellow smudge of substitute used to block the hole in the hull, which is only one of many caused by the *Bismarck's* guns, when the Catalina suddenly appeared out of cloud only fifteen hundred feet over her prow. At the time of the attack, they had to stop up the damage with whatever materials they had handy, and what do you think they did use for the largest hole of all? Their margarine ration!

But let's start at the beginning of the story as it was recounted to me by the crew themselves.

At a quarter past two they were told last Sunday night, or rather last Monday morning, that there was an operation for them. Within three-quarters of an hour they were on board in the loch, waiting for the signal from the Aldis lamp that would flash in the darkness from the topmost turret of a nearby hill. Think of them as they waited for the signal in the remote isolated darkness. . . .

Altogether there were ten on board. Three of them were close friends who had already flown together for hundreds of hours, one from New Barnet, another from Liverpool, the third from Newcastle, the wireless operator whose destiny it was to tap out that precious, vital signal. To each other, they were Tich, Eddie and Marco.

Then there was a rigger from Chadley, another member of the crew came from Romford, and yet another from Mayfield in Sussex, while as for the two pilots, one has already had a piece of outstanding good fortune in the war, for he had been a member of the original crew of the first Catalina to operate in the Battle of the Atlantic, had crashed, and been saved to fight again. Saved to bring off a scoop of the first magnitude. While his co-pilot I found was an old friend of mine. We had met several months previously at another station, which is described in Chapter Three of this section. I knew so well what he must have been thinking of in that last moment before they were air-borne . . . of his parents, caught in Jersey, and of whom he had no news since the German occupation . . . and of the little village in the Cotswolds where his wife lives . . . Guiting Tower. As far removed from war as the beauty of the rhododendrons now hidden by the blanket of night. And their thoughts, too. But all the same I would take a bet that all the crew had one thought in common—the motto of their squadron—" Seek and Follow."

And then they were off. . . .

The first three hours, they told me, are always the worst. You would have expected them to say the last three hours of their eighteen-hour trip, but no, they were emphatic it was the first three. After that, they settle down to a routine, they added. The routine consists of three hours on watch, and one hour off, when they take it in turns to lie down on one of the four bunks aft.

After the first three hours, on this occasion, the dawn came and they had an excuse to break the monotony by cooking their breakfast of bacon and eggs on a primus stove. When I asked them what struck them most about the trip, they assured me in chorus that it was the long wait before they had their lunch. And we usually have our meals so regularly, they continued.

Things weren't so regular this time.

When they sighted the *Bismarck* and sent the miraculous message back to their base, the wireless operator from Newcastle told me that it took him three minutes to transcribe. Three minutes. But it seemed like eternity to him, because all the time they were being attacked, weaving and rocking in a kind of perpetual crazy pattern—And what did you do? I asked. . . . Oh, we shot back at them . . . talk of David and Goliath. And even when the wireless operator had tapped out the last letter, his troubles were not over yet, because just as he was sitting back thankfully, holding on to his seat as the machine took evasive action, he was asked, if you please, over the air from Headquarters, to repeat !

The truth was, the folks at home in the Ops room thought it was too good to be true. Indeed, I heard afterwards that when this Catalina set out on patrol, someone had the bright idea in the Ops room of betting a sergeant rigger twenty cigarettes that they would never find the *Bismarck*. And as twenty cigarettes are more valuable than a rope of pearls in that isolated outpost, I only hope he has remembered by now to pay up. Actually the second pilot told me himself that he could hardly believe his eyes when he saw the enemy battleship beneath them. It was the size of a cigar box, he said, no bigger, and so well camouflaged with light blue paint that it was extremely difficult to follow with the eye, even from a quarter of a mile away.

After they had sent the two signals back and been forced by the fierceness of the attack to take to their wings and escape back into cloud, they lost sight of the *Bismarck*, but not long afterwards they ran into their sister Catalina that had been ordered to do a sweep next to them. And as the boy in the crew, whose home is in New Barnet, put it : " We formated on her for a bit, and I could have hugged her, I was so bucked and excited."

And that was why they were so late having their lunch. It was only friendly to keep guard over their sister, manning all their guns, because she had been threatened by an attack by four fighters catapulted from the *Bismarck's* deck.

I nearly forgot about that, and it is very important. For it shows just how desperate the *Bismarck's* captain was, and moreover, how near he was to escaping. There can be no doubt about those fighters, though I have seen no reference to them in the official account. But the pilot of the second Catalina is quite positive that he saw the black crosses on their wings. And he ought to know. Yet the fact remains that when those fighters left the deck of their mother ship, they were committing suicide just as openly as when a man deliberately jumps off a precipice.

One must pay tribute to the self-discipline of the enemy : to be catapulted off into the skies, knowing that you would never be able to land again, because the ship dare not slow down, to impede its escape, but taking off, just the same, and believing it to be worth-while, if only they could send crashing into the sea our two planes before they had time to despatch a signal to their base. And how nearly they succeeded. I saw for myself when I climbed into the cockpit and stared down at the freshly mended wound.

Back at Headquarters again, the C.O. of the station said something to me which I think is important, and should be remembered on all future occasions when one is reading of the further exploits of these machines which come to us by the courtesy of a great band of American workers in San Diego. The group captain reminded me of two things. First, how much more cramped the Catalina crews are compared with those who fly in the Sunderlands. I know from the experience which I described in my last book, that life on a Sunderland, were it not for the dangers of patrol, is almost luxurious. There is a mess deck. You sit down to your meals, as though you were in the saloon of a smart yacht. You can lie down, too, and sleep or read *No Orchids for Miss Blandish*, and at the most, you are only sea-borne for twelve or fourteen hours.

Whereas a Catalina, carrying no less than fifteen hundred gallons of petrol, can stay in the air for twenty hours, and even more if pressed. On the other hand, it is only a single decker, there is no space to move around, no mess deck for meals, no illusion even of some modicum of comfort, yet at the same time, you endure the same intense vibration and continuous cacophony of sound as a member of a Sunderland crew. Indeed, my friend the second pilot was still wearing cotton wool in his ears from the last trip.

And now they are ready to be off again . . . thanks to the maintenance staff, who took it in turns to stand for two hours at a time in the icy waters of the loch, right up to their chins, to finish off the job of plugging up the hole in

(*Above*) Some of the crew of the British tug, *Freebooter*. That's a name to make the ghostly drum of Drake roll again, I thought.

(*Below*) Bunts's father is Mine Host of the Royal Oak at Weybridge. "Any time you are passing, there's a glass of beer on the House," he assured me.

the hull, and thereby keeping the Catalina in commission. When the damage that had been done to her was checked over, she was about to be sent to a repair base a long way off, but the ground staff volunteered to become divers for two days, so that the flying boat could be kept on the spot, and be ready that much quicker for patrol work again. And I think that should be recorded in the official story of this historic search, too. It is only one more proof that a man does not necessarily have to wear wings upon his tunic to demonstrate that he is deserving of his countrymen's approbation.

In case this diary of mine ever crosses the Atlantic, I thought it might be of interest to record for the benefit of the workers in a certain aeroplane factory in San Diego, exactly what these sergeant riggers have to say about this latest contribution to the war effort of Coastal Command. They said in chorus : " She's as smooth as a sewing machine to work and her engines stay put just as automatically. And actually, the other day, she proved the worth of her engines when another Catalina in this squadron, out on patrol, had to come back five hundred miles on one engine."

The Catalina which first sighted the *Bismarck* returned to her base at nine-thirty at night, and the crew told me that it was exactly like Cowes Regatta. Every motor-boat in the loch sped towards the buoy to cheer lustily and also to stand by and give help in case the hole in the hull caused her to sink like a stone to the bottom of the loch when she hit the water.

That must have been a tricky moment for the two pilots. As soon as they were seaborne again safely, they climbed out and went off to the operations room to report. And do you know, despite their reception from the " regatta," they went very shyly and nervously into the room because they expected to have a strip torn off them. When my friend suggested that, I gazed at him in astonishment. But he was not kidding ; he was absolutely genuine about it.

H.B.D.

He continued : " You see, although we found the *Bismarck* originally, we lost sight of her again when we had to take evasive action, and our orders were to shadow her all day long, even if it was ten-tenths cloud."

And that brings me to the second point which the group captain had impressed upon me. How day in and day out, in all weathers, in all conditions, these Coastal Command planes do their job looking after convoys, searching for submarines, taking reconnaissance pictures, patrols that are so often dull and monotonous and ordinary people like you and I only hear about their routine when something tremendous happens like the sinking of the *Bismarck* through their assistance. But that is only one day's work to them. Why, the squadron of Hudsons with whom I did my trip over Norway has at the moment of writing just completed its millionth hour of operations and during the whole course of the war there has not been a single day when Coastal Command has not operated in some capacity or other, a record unequalled by any branch of the Services. And altogether, they have flown a distance which is more than half-way to the sun.

And because through having flown with them so much in this war, I feel very strongly that their personnel deserves a place in the sun, I want to end this chapter again by coming back to the crew, who at this moment are waiting in a hut, barren of all comfort except their dormitory beds, waiting for the next trip. Once more they are " on strike," though I hasten to explain that that does not suggest what it would in a factory. It means simply that though they can lie down in their clothes and try to sleep, they must be ready to leave again at three-quarters of an hour's notice, as they were a few nights ago.

What did you do when you got back that night ? I asked them. How did you celebrate ? Well, said one, and another nodded his agreement, we went and had a drink in the mess. Surely someone offered you a drink, I suggested. At that they all grinned and shook their heads. Good heavens, no, it was all in a day's work. We wouldn't have expected a free drink even if we had sunk the ship ourselves.

I said nothing. There was nothing I could say. Instead, I looked down on the bed round which we were all standing in a group, and there on the counterpane, was the wicker basket containing their rations for the next trip. Two loaves of bread, some meat, an egg each and the usual carrots and potatoes. All done up neatly in packages as for a picnic. What a picnic, I thought.

Chapter Three

THE BOMBER PILOT OF TO-MORROW

You are forced to make a precautionary landing.
Choose your own field and take your own time. One
of your engines has failed. . . .

WE ARE in the air, flying steadily above the rich, heavy Cotswold earth, our own training Anson multiplied and reflected as in a dozen-faced mirror by all the other similar craft, scattered and silhouetted against the pale light of the afternoon, like bees, going to and fro from the honey pot to the hive of the aerodrome, now disappearing on the horizon behind us.

At first, from my seat behind the dual control, it was difficult to tell which was the instructor, which the pupil, perfecting his training, as the bomber pilot of to-morrow. Their flying helmets, their brown-yellow flying suits were identical, neither showed any trace of nerves or inexperience by the set of their shoulders. It had been like any other trip until the fellow on the right spoke in his soft Canadian voice.

Then as the pupil calmly made a couple of dummy runs before coming down, I suddenly remembered what I had seen written up in capitals on the wall of his squadron commander's office : YOUR ARRIVAL SHOULD BE MERELY THE END OF A JOURNEY AND NOT THE END OF EVERYTHING.

And I thought, too : he is getting to the end of another journey now. The journey which started many months ago, when, as a cadet, he went to his I.T.W. (Initial Training Wing) and from there to his E.F.T.S. (Elementary Flying Training School) where he first was allowed to fly, and now he is almost at the end of his course at the S.F.T.S. (Service Flying Training School) where not only is he in the air by day but some of the time is devoted to night flights and landing, going solo at the last.

And of course, there are the lectures, a hundred and sixty hours of them, as well as the lessons in the sky in formation flying, low flying—once when we were skirting a hillside thick with firs, our instructor, I noticed, made a sharp movement with his hand, not at the controls, but above, to warn him to bring his plane round and quickly—while he has been going off on cross-country flights up to three hundred miles, without an instructor, taking it in turns with a fellow-cadet, to be pilot or navigator.

He finds the navigating tests, both in the exam. room and in practical experience, the most difficult of all his fences. And when I say " he," I am not thinking simply of the boy with whom I flew, who this time last year was farming, but of *all* the fifty volunteers in his course. After flying with them and talking with them and playing squash with them, and staying in their mess for several days, this is the portrait as I see it.

But it is a picture based not simply on the snapshot you see of us, taken after our trip together, but a composite portrait of all of them. I want to make that very clear. Such a portrait is possible, because they all feel the same. They may have come into the Air Force from Oxford, or Smithfield Market, have just left a public school like Radley, or been serving their apprenticeship in a Bournemouth bank, but they all feel the same about the job ahead of them, about the part they are destined to play in the great bombing offensive that is an essential prelude to victory.

They want to be bomber pilots because they believe
that that is the quickest way to end the war. They may
look younger than their average age of twenty years, they
may have a scrum in the mess to get hold of the only copy
of *The Saint Omnibus*, they may quench their thirst in nothing
stronger than shandy, they may not be allowed to keep a
motor-bike and be supposed to be in their rooms by ten-
thirty, but when one of them in the mess reads out the
latest casualty figures from the Russian front, you see the
same look in all their eyes. And you have only to watch
them at bombing practice to realize the intensity and
single-heartedness of their feeling.

One day they fly ; the next day they stay on the
ground. He—all of them—prefers the flying naturally,
but he realizes that the ground work must be covered,
too, and exciting things can happen on the ground.
There is, for instance, the Link Trainer, and the Bombing
Teacher.

To attend a session, you go through a door in one of
the main buildings, up some stairs, and find yourself on a
balcony rather like the spectator's gallery of a squash court.
The space below you, though, is only twelve feet, and on
its surface is thrown the black and white reflection of a
composite photograph of a typical landscape. Just behind
me in the dim light—like that of a photographer's dark-
room—is the captain of the airplane, sitting on a kitchen
chair, while in front of him lying full length on his stomach
as in a month or two's time he may be lying on the belly
of a Wellington—he said he hoped to be posted to a
Wellington Station—is his co-pilot, taking bombing aim.
The instructor, on the extreme right of us, where the gallery
reaches down the side of the wall, points with a long stick
to a spot down below, and the shadow from his pointer is
reflected across the landscape. That is your target, he tells
him. There is a camouflaged factory behind those trees.
Ready? Remember, red on red. . . .

Red on red . . . every pupil, every pilot with wings

on his tunic must wake sometimes in the night, muttering those three words in a dream. Red on red . . . for that means all the difference between a plumb hit on your target, and the waste of your valuable cargo on a bombing raid. You see, to be certain of hitting his target, a bomb aimer must make due allowance for wind speed and direction. To take a drift, he places the N point of the bearing plate over the red compass needle of his bombsight compass, and the angle thus recorded is correctly orientated with magnetic north. Putting north on north is called Red on Red in the Service . . . and it must be damnably easy in the excitement of the attack sometimes to forget. . . .

We are at ten thousand feet, and travelling at two hundred miles, and he knows that he's got to release his bomb at a mile and seven hundred yards before we reach the target, which seems now to be starting to move towards us. Silence in the microcosm except for his directions to his pilot behind him. Left . . . steady . . . right . . . steady . . . RIGHT . . . the landscape turns on an arc below us . . . your own breath catches in excitement . . . as he announces : Bomb released. . . .

A second later, below us on the floor comes into sight a circle like the firing target of a shooting range, with an illuminated cross in the centre of the bull's-eye. Will it come to a standstill over the heart of the objective ? Each of those outer rings counts as thirty yards. Hmn. Afraid I only smashed a few windows, he mutters.

We start again : sometimes he chooses his own target. Always the instructor explains in simple, friendly language, why the bomb has fallen to the left or right, short or in advance. But at last he records a plumb hit bang on the middle and I can't help asking him where he would have liked that bomb to have fallen, and there is no mistaking the fervour of his voice as he answers : Berlin every time. Whereupon the whole process of make-believe assumes a sudden meaning and reality which will stay with me as long as my memory of the reiterated warning . . . Red on Red. . . .

METHOD MAY TAKE TIME, BUT IT IS BETTER TO BE LATE,
MR. AIRMAN, THAN THE LATE MR. AIRMAN.

That reminder has also caught his eye on the wall
many times in the course of his final training these last few
weeks. Its meaning came home to me when they showed
me a lecture room, where on the day that they are on the
ground, two by two the Cadets take it in turns to practise
in the Link Trainer. There it stands on a pedestal, upon
an arrangement of giant bellows which can even simulate
a realistic reproduction of Bumpy Weather. The stubby,
foreshortened toy machine, all blue and silver, reminds you
of something on a stand at the exhibition at Olympia. But
it is there for a much more serious reason. It is there to
teach every pilot how to subjugate his own ego, to override
the instinct all human beings have for imagining they themselves know best, rather than to put their complete trust
in the unfailing regularity of scientific instruments.

When he climbs into the cockpit, the roof shuts over
him, he can see nothing from that moment onwards. He
is alone in a way that only an airman flying blind can be
alone as in the next half-hour he is put through perhaps
the most unpleasant of all aerial manœuvres, the job of
flying on a blind course, and making if necessary, a perfect
Lorentz landing in a ground fog, at the end of the journey.

The C.O. of the station happened to be standing there
beside the officer, giving wireless instructions from the table
on which the graph of the pupil's course in the air is recorded
in red ink parabula by parabula. The C.O. was saying :
" Often in the air you think you are going one way but
really you are going quite another, you think you are
gaining height and you are losing rapidly. Once he has got
into the habit of surrendering himself to his instruments,
really trusting his artificial horizon and glueing his eyes on
it more than half the battle is won."

Afterwards they took me for a ride myself, and the graph
of my progress you see reproduced with this chapter. I
started off all right, but that squiggle at the end is, I am
afraid, a spin which looks very much like a final one. In

chorus the two pupils, veterans to me, spoke words of comfort. " It wasn't fair to put on bumpy weather for you the first time," they said.

One of those two pilots of to-morrow had a white armlet on his jacket ; that means that when he passes on to his Operational Training Unit, where the final stage of all is reached, and he becomes a member of a crew working together, he will go as a Pilot Officer, his friend at his side, as a Sergeant.

But make no mistake about it. There is no kind of distinction created because of his school or the games he plays, or his peacetime background. This final promotion at the end of many months' training for a certain percentage of the cadets is based entirely on results, and you can appreciate the high standards of the course and the teaching when I tell you that in his Wings Exam, which he has just passed, he was only eleventh, though his percentage was 81, and even the cadet who passed out thirty-third has reached over 70 per cent.

Exam results ? The D.F.C.'s of to-morrow will have to find his wings through other qualities than passing exams. That is true, but again make no mistake. Most important of all was his Flight Commander's report which said of him : " A keen type. Quick to learn, has no special faults."

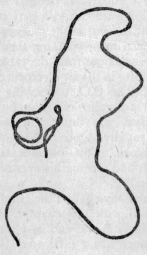

Until the war is over, every volunteer for flying duties who sets out to earn such a report, has just as much chance of promotion. And the more time I spend with the R.A.F. the more I realize that this Service sets an example to the whole world in the meaning of true democracy.

The story of this voyage will go down in the history of the war as an epic achievement.

ASPICE ET IMITARE. Look and imitate and in the centre
the torch of knowledge. It is the crest of the station, reproduced in the hall of the mess and every time the cadets pass
through on their way to meals they must see it. Their
own instructor may well have been trained here only a year
ago and now wears the D.F.C. upon his own tunic. There
was one such there whom I had met at Cambridge just
before the war, a member of the Committee of the Varsity
Union. During the debate in which I was speaking, I
remember envying and marvelling at their undergraduate
self-confidence and wondering how long it would last when
they went out into the world. And now I have a new memory
to replace that one. I shall remember him saying to me :
" The worst fault we ever find among chaps we are training
is not packing up through nerves—they are marvellously
free from that—but over-confidence. And there is no way
of curing that except . . ."

But there is one moment of confidence when he is on
top of the world that no one would begrudge him, no one
try to take from him. The moment when he knows that
he has won the right to wear a pair of wings upon his
tunic.

On my last evening as their guest I went into one of
the huts on the camp and found him sitting at the table in
front of his school-study fire, smoking a pipe, and sending
off Christmas cards, with the wings of the R.A.F. embossed
upon them. As though he could guess what was in my
mind, he suddenly went to the cupboard and out of it he
took his best tunic and there was the badge again but now
it had assumed a new glory, there upon the left breast a
shining new pair of wings.

He must wait another week or so before he wears that
tunic, the day he passes out from the Training School.
Meanwhile he can only gaze upon it in the secrecy of his
own room. He said : " I sewed them on myself, it took
me hours, I have never sewed anything in my life before,
but I was told that it would bring me luck. I bought them
in the nearest town. They only had the 2s. sort. I believe

you can pay as much as 6s. when they are all silvered up. But I guess these are good enough to be going on with "

I guess so, too   You see, there are still some things in the world which can't be bought.

Chapter Four

TAIL-END CHARLIE

" IF "

" If you cotton on to tracer
    And harmonize your gun,
Systemically sky search,
    Especially in the sun.
If you're good at recognition
    Of aircraft friend or foe,
Can estimate 400 yards
    And think you really know
The sighting that's required,
    A long but steady burst.
If you can do all that, my lad,
    Then Fritz will come down first."

THEY call him " Tail-end Charlie," and you see a snapshot I took of him the other day, climbing out of the rear gun turret of a Whitley. The picture of an air gunner, just finishing his training. But this is a portrait in words, not of one particular fellow, but of all of them, all those who were rookies a few months ago, and now by the time you reach this chapter, will be flying over Germany by night in the tail end of a bomber.

He has come from the ends of the world to play his part. He is nearer twenty than thirty, five foot six than six feet ; he has a chin that you keep on noticing over and over again and strongly marked eyebrows. He wears his cap an inch above the right eye, he has taught himself to prefer chewing gum to cigarettes because he cannot smoke in the air ; he drinks hardly at all and when he says that so-and-so has gone for a Burton, he means that he went off on an operational trip and did not come back.

When I had tea with him in his mess—fish-cake and chips—round me crowded volunteers from Brazil and New Zealand and Jersey; a boy of twenty-one from Bannockburn, who a year ago was working in an outfitter's shop in Stirling; another boy from Bromley who was a builder, a third who was an insurance inspector from Liverpool and a fourth who used to be a school teacher and admitted that once upon a time, he used to swear he could not sit with his back to the engine in a train because it made him feel sick . . .

In the past, there had been a false idea that air gunners are tough guys made of bone from the neck up. They are tough all right, but it is a toughness of the mind as much as of the body. What has divided them from being pilots has been a lack of knowledge of mathematics rather than a lack of general intelligence.

When I asked him why he had volunteered to be an air gunner, he did not suggest it was because he becomes a sergeant at the end of his training and gets 10s. 6d. a day flying pay, but instead he said simply: It's good to know that you are behind four guns I imagined he was remembering what an instructor, with the D.F.M. on his tunic, had been pointing out with some insistence that afternoon. Don't set out to be brave, he said in the lecture room, but to be efficient, so efficient that the rest follows automatically.

Every time I visit a fresh aspect of R.A.F. Training Command, my final impression is always the same, that nothing has been left to chance in the perfecting of the collaboration between the pupil and his instruments. At the Station which we are visiting in this chapter, out on the marshes, they have set up a wonderful new invention, a training toy for air gunners, a little like a greyhound track, which cost five thousand pounds and is likely to save, before the war is over, more than that number of lives.

Instead of the hare, you see coming towards you, two

hundred yards away, a wooden model of a Messerschmitt suspended above the track, rather like a giraffe's head. Charlie sits in a reproduction of a real gun turret and pots at the target as it comes towards him, as it is opposite, and as it is going away down the track again in retreat.

I tried my hand at it and found I scored more direct hits with the scarlet tracer bullets when the model was going away from me. But Charlie said he found it easiest to take aim when it was coming towards him. You see, he added, I know then that it must be either him or me. I do not know whether that was grammatical, it was certainly graphic. And above us, as he spoke, as though to give a final reality to what was in his mind, there suddenly wheeled against the winter afternoon, a great flight of wild duck, darkening the sky like Messerschmitts out on patrol.

This afternoon, it may well be that you will stop digging in your garden for a moment and crane your neck to watch a flight of our bombers going off to do their job, with their great wings outstretched, and there in the tail, catching the last glow of the sunset, like a tiny brilliant jewel, the rear gun turret. Think of the turret's solitary watcher. His job for the next eight hours is hardly a jewel. Have you tried to imagine what it is like up there, how much space he has, how he manages to keep awake and warm? Come with me, and you may understand a little better. Charlie and a couple of friends and myself went out on exercises together over the sea. There's plenty of room for you in the fuselage to sit on the floor beside me, while we are waiting our turn to go into the turret and practise shooting at a Drogue target, towed by a Battle.

What strikes you at once, what must have struck him, too, the first time he climbed into a Whitley, is the great distance from the pilot's quarters to his own rear seat with his back to the engine. Eighty steps or more it takes you before you reach the bulkhead door, six feet from the turret itself, and that is your parting place from the rest of the crew. You push that door open and the warmth of companionship is gone, and a great wind hits you and you know that hereafter, till the end of the trip, you are imprisoned in solitary confinement, without room to move your arms, with your head touching the ceiling of your glass cell.

When I climbed through the hatch myself, on the shooting range high up over the sea, the instructor behind me used the same admonitions that he had done so many times to Charlie, reminding me to put up my two hands on to those two straps—just like straps in a Tube car—and thus aided, you slide into the turret, legs first. There's not room to get in any other way.

Your first reaction is how different it is from sitting beside the pilot ; not because you are alone, not because you are looking the other way now, but simply because of the wobble of the turret, as it rocks slightly in the slipstream. Charlie told me himself that at first he could not believe that he was still in part of the machine. He thought instead that he was being towed himself, like being towed in a ball of glass behind a racing motor careering round Brooklands, yes, but not on the ground, but thousands of feet in the air. Perhaps that is why the air gunners have readapted the R.A.F. motto to themselves. They say : *Per Ardua ad Terramfirmam.*

He is firm enough, anyway, on his seat in the turret, fixed in tight with his knees up against the ammunition tanks, his back against the doors, which he has taken good care to lock before turning on the switch which sets the power turret free to rotate. Just in front of him, close to his stomach, are the two handles which combine the levers for moving the turret to left or to right, with the triggers for shooting his four Browning guns. The combination is so neat, so compact, that to gyrate the tower, you only have to move the handles sideways, just as you would swing the bars of a bicycle and with no more effort.

On a line with your eyes are the reflector sights, and before you shoot at the Drogue—understudy for the enemy —floating behind the Battle, like a parachute rolled up with a black band round the centre of it, you move your head forward to get the target bang in that circle of light on the reflector, and there is a pad for you to press your right cheek against, to be certain that your head is in position.

That rubber pad is somehow pleasant and reassuring. But perhaps, after you have had your cheek against it for several hours, your reaction is not so good, especially when, as one veteran gunner told me, the searchlights catch you and you desperately wriggle your head from side to side to try to escape. It is as though someone had suddenly placed sheets of white wallpaper all round your turret, that Charlie said.

And how do you keep awake, how do you keep warm? I persisted. You keep warm, he replied, by raising your knees the couple of inches you can, up and down, up and down, up and down. And you keep yourself awake because you have been told : TO BE SURPRISED IS TO BE LOST.

That goes round and round in his brain like a jingle because it has been impressed upon him over and over again how the rest of the crew depend on him for their safety. He has been warned, too, to fire an opening burst at six hundred yards from the enemy, so that the tracer will give him a line of fire, and then to hold his ammunition until the enemy come within range from four hundred yards onwards.

You see the special version of Rudyard Kipling's " If " at the head of this chapter. He's learned that off by heart, too. And about night operations, he has learned something else ; how his chances are best of all if he foxes the enemy into imagining that he has not seen him until he is at point-blank range of two hundred yards or even less. Then he gives him all he's got, while at that range, the enemy cannot used his cannon with accuracy.

That is pukka gen. What does that mean? It's his slang for " Information from a reliable source worth remembering." Other pukka gen concerns his wireless training. Before he came to the station where he is taking his final gunnery course, he has spent many weeks mastering wireless, so that he will be of the maximum use to the captain of his aircraft. On a long journey, he and the wireless operator sometimes exchange places halfway through. Or again, if anything happens to the wireless operator, he can take over.

Duff gen is the opposite of pukka gen ; it is handed out by chaps who suggest to him that he should not be a slurge, that the local dance hall is the place to spend his evenings. A slurge is a swot. But it is a good thing to be a slurge when you are in training. So if any one suggests : Come on, let's have an evening with the jeeps, he replies, Wind your neck in. That means : Shut up. Girls can come later.

Meanwhile, he does not forget to write home, almost every day, he told me, and in his last letter, he was describing flying in the rear seat of a Battle, firing down at a stationary target on the sands. The target consists of four large wooden letters spaced out, A, B, C, D. What do those letters stand for in his imagination as he fires ? When I tried myself, I was so busy aiming, suspended there in mid-air, standing up to fire, the letters were just the target, but in his letter home, he told his family that they stood for : Arise, Britain, Challenge the Dictators.

His own part in the challenge is so very near now. The day that he passes out, his C.O. has a talk to him about the future and I would like to quote something from that talk. You will see why in a moment. Looking forward, his C.O. says to Charlie : " You may have been flying over Germany all night, but when you descend from your aircraft on the tarmac, you are not a god descending from the clouds to honour those on the ground with your gracious presence. You have done your job—and well, we hope. So has the airman whose feet have never left the ground whilst you have been on safari, bomb strafing, or boche-hunting.

Go to it, then. Remember the Battle of Britain. What the fighter pilots did then—you can do now. The record of the other Commands so far leaves no doubt about that. You are now in the limelight, a fierce limelight which will show up any defects. in your mental, moral or physical armour. You are Non-commissioned Officers. Try to be always worthy in every way of your rank. Carry on Sergeants. Watch your step AND your stripes.

There is nothing that I can add to that, except to wish Charlie all the luck that is going, and to remind him that when he sews his brevet on to his tunic, there is already a tradition among air gunners that you leave an inch between your left breast pocket and that precious half-wing with the letters AG in the circle beside it.

What do you leave the space for ? Why, for the D.F.M., of course.

Chapter Five

THE MAN WITH ONE WING

HE only wears half a wing upon his tunic. You may have wondered what that stood for, and the O attached to it. You may have even asked him when would he finish his training and get the other half to make a pair of wings. And when he replied simply that he had finished, that he was now an air observer, since it would be shooting a line to point out that he had already done at least a dozen operational trips, he let it pass when you continued airily : Oh . . . one of those fellows who spend their nights watching for enemy aircraft coming in over the coast. Oh yes, I know . . .

But we don't know. It is extraordinary how ignorant many of us, including myself, are in regard to the exact duties of an air observer. And since in official circles, he is coming to be regarded more and more as almost the most important member of a bombing crew, I thought I'd better find out for myself and try to draw a portrait of him, both on the ground and in the air.

So not long ago, I went off and flew with him for several days on manœuvres, just when he was finishing and

They want to be bomber pilots because they believe that that is the quickest way to end the war.

passing out from his combined navigation-cum-gunnery-cum-bombing course. Yes, he has to do all that. It is he who, as soon as the machine has left the ground, gives his pilot the course to steer and continues to make a frequent check of the accuracy of his captain's course, height and air speed. Even to the extent of reminding the pilot in regard to what height he can safely come down through cloud. Again, it is he who, when his Stirling or Blenheim has come in plumb over the target, drops the bombs. So next time you hear an account, say, on the wireless, of how " we dropped our bombs on Kiel," don't imagine that the pilot at the crucial moment took one hand off his controls and pressed a button, and automatically the target was straddled.

Instead, think of that boy with the half-wing on his tunic, lying full length on his stomach in the nose of the machine, sweating in the last seconds before zero hour. With your own inter-com. plugged in, you can hear what he is saying to the pilot. Attack. Target sighted. Attack. Left. *Left*. (The machine swings a little.) Steady. And then a second later—Bomb released.

Together we flew out over the Irish Sea in a Botha and I watched him drop eight bombs on a floating wooden target, a thirty-foot triangle which looked the size of a match-box from the air. And each time he pressed the rubber button on the end of the cord, he wriggled his legs and I heard him mutter something extra into his inter-com. . . . That goes for London . . . and that for Liverpool . . . and that for Bristol. . . .

I don't know if that improved the accuracy of his aim which was remarkably good, but I can tell you that even dropping a dummy bomb gives you a great kick, because when he had had his quota, he generously allowed me to take his place on the floor of the fuselage and have a crack myself. As you lie there, at first it seems that the target coming down the drift wires of your bomb sight towards you, will never reach you ; then suddenly it is on you at a gallop, firmly imprisoned in the centre of the foresight and the backsight. And you squeeze the button frantically with your left hand and think of Berlin.

I was told that the bomb aimer has to fight a tendency to let off his bombs too late, to wait too long. I was told, too, that at ten thousand feet, travelling at two hundred miles an hour, your bomb falls three hundred feet a second, and to obtain a direct hit, you actually release it a mile and a half before you reach your target, though in the air, you seem to be more than over it, almost beyond.

Through an escape trap, I stared downwards at the bombs as they fell. First they seemed to flash forwards, sunlit and silvered, as though they were actually flying level with the aircraft, and then down, down, diminishing into dots. The veterans assure you that when flak comes up at your machine, at first it seems to travel inordinately slowly, and then the last two thousand feet, to be propelled with a sudden jerk as though it were on a piece of catapult. In reverse ration, the bomb on its descent seems to drop very swiftly at first, and then to stay poised in the air, so that you begin to panic that you will be miles past the target before it reaches sea level.

Now I am leaning over the bomb aimer's shoulder. And something in me records that he is staring out and down, through a piece of glass, shaped by the fabric joins of the machine to exactly the same size as an ordinary dressing-table mirror. That comparison, that contrast, once evoked, stays in your mind. All these fellows finishing their training and the various mirrors in which they must have knotted their so different ties every morning in civvy street. And now one universal, black tie.

I was told by the chief instructor at one school I visited, that even the idea that in order to become an air observer you have to be a wizard at maths, isn't " pukka gen." All that is required is average maths and average intelligence. The rest is concentration, good will and guts. Among them I discovered every type, from a rancher from the Argentine to a professor of music from the Royal Academy, and a repertory actor who volunteered it was not nearly such hard work as learning a new part every week. There were men of thirty-two and thirty-three, who had been their own boss and built up their own businesses in peacetime ; there were boys of nineteen fresh from the Varsity. His average age, then, is about twenty-five. I think you would notice the difference at once between him and an air gunner or a bomber pilot. On the whole, he is taller than the former and not so thick-set, while he has a more serious expression in his eyes and a more rumpled forehead than the latter. And no wonder !

One sergeant instructor, now lecturing in the school, as a so-called rest after thirty operational flights, explained to me that from the time you leave your base until you return, maybe nine or ten hours later, there is not a single moment when the observer can relax, except possibly when crossing the sea between the coast of England and Holland or France. They always say, he added caustically, that if we have a spare moment, we can polish the brasswork.

"But don't forget, though in a bomber there are often two pilots, two wireless ops, and two gunners, there is never more than one navigator, whose job it is to keep the only log of the trip, as well as all the rest of his duties, and he has to keep that up to date, minute by minute, or else when he lands, it will be a case of too many cooks spoil the chart. And on my way back, it is no use when the captain asks on the inter-com. : Where are we ?—replying, "God alone knows, somewhere over the North Sea." That is why the brasswork is always so dirty ! "

This particular observer, strangely enough, said that he had not minded trips over Berlin at all ; his hardest trip had been over Bordeaux, while his nearest escape was in a raid over Rotterdam, when to be certain of hitting their target, his machine had, as he put it graphically, come right down under the umbrella of flak.

Thus and thus they pass on the fruit of their experience. One aerodrome that I visited has been nicknamed " the

Station of Blue Magic," because it is here that they have been experimenting and achieving spectacular success with every kind of gadget and " toy " that will increase the standard of efficiency in the observers of to-morrow. One of them struck me particularly as a brilliant contrivance, whose purpose is to imprint recognition of aircraft implacably upon a pupil's vision. In short, to prevent such famous last words as " I told you it wasn't a Hudson."

The back wall is like one half of the arch of a huge plaster egg. In the foreground, you sit in a turret, and on the screen at the back, is projected through the camera the silhouette of an ME. 109 F coming towards you. By the manipulation of a lever, the instructor at your side can make the aircraft flick across the screen in a realistic reproduction of an actual attack. So much so that you are certain you are in the air, you are certain it is you or the other man.

Five minutes later, you have come to earth again, you walk into a classroom and there on the blackboard, a sergeant with the D.F.M. below the half-wing on his tunic is carefully writing up the morning's problem. They call it " a dry swim." A navigation exercise on the ground, which is the equivalent of the course so soon now they will be experiencing in earnest on operations.

You are the navigator of a Wellington, he wrote. Your orders are—a daylight raid on Osnabruck. You reach the target and bomb, but owing to heavy flak, you fly off on a course of two hundred and five degrees (M), you set course at 12.30, at 12.45 you pin-point yourself at Dortmund. What is your new W-V ? (Wind Velocity).

Nothing is left to chance in his training. Increasingly is emphasis and time given to the understanding of astranavigation, which I was assured is much simpler than it sounds, and now Arcturas and Regulus, Spica and Vega are names that are engraved upon every observer's mind. Though I suppose always the letters D.R., which stand for Dead Reckoning, must remain for him the equivalent of the D.V. upon which so many of us have fallen back in times of stress.

For after all, it was by the use of D.R., when the stars were blotted out and daylight came without sun, that the navigator of the Catalina which found the *Bismarck* plotted her position so accurately that the Navy was able to take up the chase again at once.

A story that will go down in history, as I have described in detail in a previous chapter. And because of the multiplication of such stories, even those fellows who volunteered to be pilots and for some reason or other have been transferred to be trained as observers, soon cease to have any regrets, and instead become immersed in the knowledge that the thunderbolt, the boomerang, which is a modern bomber, secretly skirts the fathomless heavens and miraculously reaches its objective, through their skill, their strength.

" IT IS A GREAT STRENGTH TO BELIEVE WE CANNOT LOSE, BUT IT IS TREASON TO ACT AS THOUGH THE VICTORY WILL WIN ITSELF." On the last night of my stay among them, I walked across to the huts in which the cadets live when they are off duty, and I found those words written up on a door. So I knocked and entered, and there was a boy bending over a map, plotting his course for to-morrow's voyage, when the Station Commander was flying us over the sea.

My companion said : I wish it were Berlin, and I thought of what the wing commander himself had said to the new batch coming in that afternoon. " What you learn here will show you the way how to bomb Berlin, and how to get back to your base so as to be ready to bomb again the next day."

That was no idle boast. From now on the Germans will have to endure the assaults of hundreds of new bomber crews. And so next time you come across a fellow with half a wing on his tunic and an O beside it, don't ask him when he will finish his training and get the other half to his wings. Don't ask him anything. Just shake his hand and offer him a drink.

Chapter Six

THE BALLOON GOES UP

IT is a familiar sight in bombed London or any other of our blitzed cities. A square of tidy little houses, with their quiet even lives across the years, suddenly disrupted and laid waste. In the centre of the square, where once there were flowers and grass, now were the sad mementoes of the evacuated owners, broken pieces of furniture, books and household utensils, all in an incongruous heap, where they had been hurled outwards by the blast.

I stood there, idly looking round, and then my eyes suddenly caught something different from the usual pattern : a piece of blue cloth, the blue of an Air Force uniform. I picked it up from the ruins, and that same second my companion said : When the bombs fell one Saturday night, some of the balloon crew for this square were in their dug-out over there, and they escaped, just escaped with their lives, but two were outside, watching the cable, on duty. That was the sleeve of one of them. . . .

His voice slurred into silence. Anyway, there was no need for him to finish the sentence. You can finish it for him. Indeed, you can go further. Next time you hear any one suggest that the many thousand members of the Air Force who look after the country's balloon barrage are not on active service, you might suggest a meeting with the survivors from that balloon site. I'll gladly arrange the party.

My own eyes were opened when I had the privilege of making an extended tour of some of the sites round London. I had heard many stories of the bravery of the men who look after the balloons that accompany our coastal convoys on their tricky journeys through the Channel, and of the men in the Balloon Service, who often spend weeks at a time on drifters in the North Sea, but here were equally numerous examples of a different kind of courage. For instance, there was one site I visited on a high hill, which was surrounded by bomb craters, but all the corporal in charge had to say about it was : We have a ringside view here of every blitz over London. Whereas he might so reasonably have added : And when the blitz comes our way, we haven't the satisfaction of hitting back with a gun, like the Ack-Ack boys ; we just have to carry on, and take it. . . .

At another site, where the nearest pub was over four miles away, the fellows off duty were happily digging away on their allotments. They said they preferred that to walking nine miles for a pint. A peaceful and rural scene . . . on a summer afternoon. Yes . . . on a summer afternoon. But what about another winter . . . and last winter . . . and the winter before that . . . when often their site was hopelessly under water for weeks on end, and there they were, six men and a corporal, one hut and a hawser with a balloon on the end of it, marooned and with only monotony for their constant companion. Even with the allotments sprouting and the sun shining on the silver back of their Betsy, after half an hour you were not sorry to get into the car and drive away.

My guide wore the ribbon of the M.C. on his tunic, for his gallantry in the last war as a pilot. Now he has come back to the Service to do another job, which must be done, and done well. It can't be so exciting for him, and yet his enthusiasm and his efficiency caught hold of you. Never once did he remind me that in days of peace he had been a musical-comedy star and that I had last seen him on the stage at the Gaiety. But he did tell me a story that was worthy of Leslie Henson.

The story is of an old lady who came to the gate of one of these sites and inquired how long the man in the balloon stayed up there in the sky. Oh, he comes down for his dinner . . . he'd never miss his dinner, she was told. Whereupon the sentry turned away. He forgot about the old lady. But two hours later she returned. He hasn't come down yet and it's past his dinner-time, she announced triumphantly. The boy refused to be nonplussed. Oh, once a week he takes some sandwiches up to save the cook, he replied.

Actually, one human creature has gone up in a balloon since the war. That creature was a cat, who unseen crawled one day into the balloonet, the under part of the balloon, which is filled with air and not gas. Presumably she thought she had found a new and comfortable retreat for her latest accouchement. For when, hours later, the balloon returned to land again, the feline population of this country had been increased by five. The name of that cat, I am sure, was Matilda. For that is the commonest nickname of the crews for their balloons. In fact, they told me that in the Dover area, they have changed the words of a certain song to : " There'll always be a Matilda." That refers to the swiftness with which they replace balloons which, from time to time, are shot down by attacks from the French coast.

Every balloon, complete with all its apparatus, costs about eight hundred pounds. That figure might well be added in a list of war weapons given to the public when they are asked each week to proffer their savings. For no one will deny that the main object of the balloon barrage since the war has been triumphantly achieved. It has prevented the streets of our cities from being dive-bombed. It was never planned as a deterrent to bombing from a height. The answer to that must always lie with our Ack-Ack batteries and our night fighters.

Incidentally, quite often balloons are pierced by pieces of shrapnel from our own batteries and are hauled down and repaired on the spot by the crews, while the barrage is in full progress. If you imagine for a moment, an eighty-foot balloon on the ground lit up by a full moon, you can also imagine what a target it must make in the sky and the risks that the crew run at such times. Again, there can be no question of a crew ever being off duty at any hour of the night. Because orders from Command may be changed twice within an hour ; for instance, if nightfighters are going up in the vicinity.

When I watched a balloon being hauled down, and then sent skywards again, I realized why in the mess, where I dined, they referred to it as a semi-inanimate object. Indeed it seemed wholly animate in its efforts at the last moment to prevent itself being bedded down. And that was a calm night. You should be here when there is a forty-mile gale at its height, one of the crew suggested. While another added : It's the last two hundred feet which is the tricky business. Then you've got to handle her like you'd play a salmon.

I also visited an administrative centre, where the gas itself is stored in long cylinders. I was amazed to hear how many millions of cubic feet are used every month. A special train brings the cylinders to the distribution point.

Here also the balloons are mended by girls in a shop where my eyes were suddenly startled to see written up in large letters above a notice on the wall the word DOPING. Heavens, I thought, has the boredom of balloons driven them to that ! Don't worry. " Doping " is the official term for all painting of aircraft or balloons. And people employed upon such work have to drink glasses of milk at fixed intervals to prevent injurious effects.

Seeing the fabric of the balloons spread out across the floor reminded me of a visit I had paid to one of our balloon factories, where I had been asked to speak at lunch-time in the canteen to the girls about the Battle of the Atlantic, as I had made so many sorties into it.

The night before a neighbouring city had had its worst blitz of the war, so in the morning I rang up the manager of the factory expecting that he would want to cancel the visit. Instead, this is what he said : Come along and see my front line troops. So I went . . . and to my astonishment I found a scene of cheerfulness and gaiety, and not a single empty seat at the canteen tables. And when the girls crowded round to chat with me afterwards, so pretty in their cretonne overalls, although not one of them had had any sleep the night before, and many of them no breakfast and only a sandwich for lunch, because there was no means at that moment for cooking, you would have never guessed it from their faces or their gay chatter.

I would like to pick out one of them and introduce her to you. Her name was Mrs. Latham, she has seven brothers serving with the Forces and has two little twin boys. That morning she had to walk eight miles to get to her work. But she had turned up on time, and in her hair she had tied a blue bow. I commented on that and she said simply : You see, it is Air Force blue. I always wear one because I feel it brings me a bit closer to the boys we are working for.

A blue bow . . . in a girl's hair . . . and a scrap of blue uniform lying among the ruins of what was once a pleasant London square . . . and day and night in the skies above our cities, the balloons riding serenely at anchor, as much a part of the panorama of the heavens as the moon and stars themselves.

There is the pattern, but do not let us ever through familiarity take it for granted or forget the work of the men and women who make this aid to security possible. And do not let us forget something else, too : that before this war is over, the balloon may go up again . . . and again.

What do I mean by that reminder exactly ? I am thinking at this moment as I wrote of a certain country district, over which no balloons float, and of a certain afternoon when I was driven there to see another part of the pattern. It was an afternoon for sitting out under the giant cedar trees, that you sensed for centuries now had provided more than shade in the summer's heat, had given too a sense of peace and security to the owners of the lovely white stone house, with its untrammelled view across the deep green of Hertfordshire.

Only twenty-five miles from London. Only twenty-five miles from the East End and the crowded back streets of Bethnal Green and Stepney and Bow, streets which in so many cases have collapsed under the successive bombings like houses of cards. You would have thought the two worlds were so remote they were more like twenty-five thousand miles apart. And yet there is a connection—and a connection with that other blitzed square and its inhabitants which I have described earlier in this chapter—a close connection of which our country can be justly proud. Because, you see, this fair lawn with the cedar trees and the pillared façade of the noble house behind them, was occupied until the day war broke out, by the Queen of England's father.

You still don't see the connection perhaps? Don't be impatient. I will explain. On the day war broke out, Lord Strathmore vacated Woolmers Park and offered it as a voluntary gesture to the Hertfordshire County Council as a Home where mothers might go and rest and have their babies and be free of worry and care. He did not stipulate what kind of mothers should occupy the room with the terra-cotta walls, where his daughter always slept when she visited him, or the day and night nursery of the two little girls who are his granddaughters, and who must have rested many times in recent summers in the shade of those same cedar trees on the lawn.

He just gave up his home . . . and the London Hospital, whose name is a beloved one, and rightly so, in the East End, staffed the Home with its trained nurses and provided a matron and a lady almoner, who asks the mothers, when they can afford it, to pay ten shillings a week while they are waiting, and if they cannot afford it, she asks nothing of them at all. And every bed is always full in the Home and over three hundred babies have been born there since the war began.

Now Woolmers Park and its occupation is only part of a giant scheme in connection with evacuation, which in Hertfordshire, at any rate, has proved triumphantly successful. There are, altogether, a dozen emergency maternity homes, set up in the district, in addition to the ante-natal and post-natal hostels and the nursery centre which takes in toddlers up to the age of five, and thus removes a problem and a weight off the mothers' minds while they are waiting for their confinement.

I had tea with some of the mothers. I enjoyed myself. They were real people. It was interesting to hear their point of view. There was Mrs. Berry, for instance, whose husband has a little general store in Bethnal Green, and she told me now how terribly badly hit the small trader has been since, with the limitation of supplies of articles like cigarettes and tinned fruit, it is always the more influential wholesale customers, the chain stores, who get first pick. " We can only keep a small supply. We must have a quick turnover, and if we can't get supplies, people like us will be ruined. . . ."

And yet, even as she talked, you felt that somehow she and her man would manage, that she had the grit in her make-up that has brought the East-Enders through successive blitzes and made my neighbour at table, Mrs. Chapman, not betray by a mark in her face or in her manner that for the last eight months, since her home was destroyed, she had slept every night in a shelter.

Next to her was a woman in a pretty cretonne house-coat, whom I liked instantly. She looked about thirty-five at the most. Her hair was nicely done, her skin was young, only the hands which held the teacup betrayed how hard she must have worked in her life. Her name was Mrs. Pollock, her husband is a poulterer in Bethnal Green, and she told me that she was awaiting her tenth child. Four of her youngest children she had evacuated to Northampton at the beginning of the war. " Are you glad you did that ? " I asked. She nodded emphatically. " It was the best thing that could ever have happened to them," she said. " They look wonderful, and I feel that after the war is over, they'll have a really good start now in life."

Up to now, she has had four boys and five girls, and she was hoping that her new baby would be a boy, too. But most of the mothers sitting round the table, spreading the fish-paste on their bread and butter, wanted girls. They're not so much trouble, they said. They fit in better, they're easier to dress.

One mother, Mrs. Hiscock, was calling her first child June Gloria ; another mother, Mrs. Hemington, had not made up her mind yet. Her baby had only been born a few hours before. You would never have guessed that as you stood beside her bed, and the matron, Miss Ireland, told me that Mrs. Remington had eaten as good a dinner that day as any other. Beside her bed, there was a little vase full of the sweet scent of lilies of the valley. Who gave you that ? I asked. The billeting officer, was the reply.

A tiny incident, not worth recording ? I don't agree. That bunch of flowers stands for a symbol which represents the whole relationship between the guests who are evacuees, and their hosts and hostesses, who are residents of Hertfordshire. And for that reason, I cannot help feeling that it is a tragic state of affairs that so often the mothers refuse the offers to stay down in safe billets in the country, after their babies are born, and rush back to the East End, sometimes with mortal results.

Now perhaps you begin to see the connection ? Anyway, I hope you will not turn over the page too hastily in search of greater excitements than a balloon going up. I hope you will read on a little further. Listen. In one of these maternity homes, not long ago, a mother had a baby, was proud and radiant when she was told that she had produced a perfect child, but all the same, she would not listen to those who advised her to stay down there in peace. She went back to Bethnal Green and arrived just in time for a blitz in which both she and her baby were killed.

The waste of it. The folly and the futility. Doesn't it make you angry, too ? Do you not agree with me when I suggest that there should be some compulsion by which, when the mothers have had their babies out of the danger area, that they should be kept there for the duration of the war, whether the balloon looks like going up again or not ? Are we not, after all, fighting to make the world safe for all children ?

That familiar slogan stares up at me ironically from the page. The truth is, the mothers would stay nine times out of ten, but their men want them home. You can understand that, in a way . . . after all, someone has got to look after the house, and in the back of the mothers' minds is the feeling that if they do not go back, their husbands will look elsewhere for a housekeeper. Which brings me to a debate we had at Woolmers Park about the make-up of a happy marriage, and every one of those East End mothers from Bethnal Green was agreed upon one point. The only sure way by which a marriage is certain not to founder is if the woman is willing to look upon her husband as the master. Mind you, they said in chorus, if my old man didn't order me about a bit sometimes, I should feel so strange I should think there was something up.

I am afraid I had not the courage then to tell them what now I have written here. To urge them thus and thus : however much you have given in the past, stand up to your man now. Stay in the country after your baby is born. Your child's security and future is the most important problem of all.

Perhaps you who may chance upon this chapter of my war diary, may feel it is not my business to interfere. Very well. But it is *someone's* business. And I am thinking now not only of mothers who go into a reception area to have their babies, but of those thousands of parents who very sensibly took their children into safe areas at the beginning of the war and now, in what could well be termed a suicidal stream, are drifting back again to our more vulnerable cities. And I think you would agree with me, moreover, that it *is* someone's business—who knows, perhaps yours ? —had you been with me that afternoon and left the mothers at their tea and gone down the passage with the matron and entered a room where a dozen bassinets were placed round the wall.

In peacetime this room had been a study. Now instead of quietude and the calm of books, it was filled with the sudden shrill urgent cries of a dozen babies complaining that they were hungry, as they blinked their eyes and held up their tiny, ivory hands towards a world which can give them so much . . . or so little.

I leant over the baby that had been born that morning. Aren't its clothes beautiful, the matron exclaimed as she folded back the blue blanket with its piping of pink, which had come all the way from America in one of the exquisitely packed Bundles for Britain which I had seen piled up in the hall. I nodded, but my mind was far away. I was thinking how one of these children may be destined to be the future Prime Minister of England. And the immensity of the pattern, the dark immensity of life's mystery, took possession of me for a moment, and then I forced myself back from that world beyond the clouds where to-day the silver balloons ride in serene isolation. And I heard my voice coming out with a safe, ordinary sort of remark. I heard myself suggest the perfect name for the baby born this morning. Winston . . .

Chapter Seven

GROWING THEIR WINGS AGAIN

I AM writing this in a train. It is the small hours of the morning. The hour when it is impossible to lie to yourself. I am on my way back from a Christmas party, and I have travelled altogether over four hundred miles to be present at that party. You may think it rather strange in a book devoted to the war, that I should start off a new chapter talking about a Christmas party, but I can only tell you that I shall always feel very privileged to think that I was allowed to be there. And I think you will understand why when you come to the end of the chapter. But why don't you first join me at the party yourself?

We are standing in one of the lounges of a pre-war luxury hotel on the South-west coast. The guests, who once upon a time spent their holidays criticizing each other's clothes, morals and manners, have gone, perhaps for ever. Their past presence there has no power to touch the present community ; a community apart ; a community of men who have been through the fire, who have been described for all time by Galsworthy. Do you remember ? He wrote somewhere of the crisis which comes in a man's fortune, when he may crack beneath the weight of overwhelming circumstance, and then recover and return to life, never the same man again, because something has died, something has fled, but a finer man and even a bigger man. He will have got his second wind.

From the corner where you and I are standing a little apart, we can watch the men go forward, as Father Christmas calls out the name attached to the white woollen stocking that he is fishing out of his bag. You see that fellow with the head of a Viking ? He is a squadron-leader in Coastal Command. You see how straight he walks, you would not guess how many months he has been ill because of a spinal injury, the burden of a crash.

Twice he was patched up, because he was so determined to return to the attack. He took part in the great aerial torpedo raid in September, 1940, on Cherbourg, when history will record that our Air Force finally blasted the invasion plans of that summer, during which we were so desperately hard pressed. Twice when he was flying, he was suddenly struck with a numbness in his back, so that he could move his hands, but no longer his body. But he finished the job and got his crew back to their base. Now he has won the right to a long rest. He will not accept it. His one thought is to be with his squadron again.

And now you see behind him the man who cannot walk so upright towards Father Christmas because of his crutches. Look at him carefully. Would you know from his face, his walk, that like Squadron-Leader Bader, he has lost both his legs ? I didn't. His face is serene, smiling, immaculately controlled. Father Christmas says in his gruff voice : Hmm. I don't think I know your name. Have you been here long ?

A great roar of laughter goes up from the other patients

They call him " Tail End Charlie " and you see the snapshot I took of him climbing out of the rear-gun turret of a Whitley.

in their blue uniform, and the nurses standing beside them. They have guessed now the secret that Father Christmas is the medical C.O. of this R.A.F. hospital. They know, too, just how long this pilot has been there, mending.

And he can still make a joke of it all. He can still tell me that he is the only man who has ever wooed the planet of Venus with a signalling lamp from his aeroplane—*I gave her everything I'd got*, he said—mistaking her lustre for the recognition lights of a fellow-voyager in the dark and rarified night. Just as another pilot can make a joke of the miracle of his being alive to-day, by recounting how, when his machine crashed, he was thrown a hundred and fifty yards and landed again up to his neck in a sewage farm, where he was found by a farmer eight hours later. But the nurses would not come near me for eight days, after that, and I don't blame them, he added.

Now we are standing beside the counter of the bar. Yes, within the hospital. A first-rate idea. A bar where the convalescent cases can have a glass of beer and pretend that they are back in their mess. It helps to heal their minds, like the debates they have every week now, with such motions as " This House is of the opinion that in war-time, woman-power should also be conscripted." And the motion was carried by thirty-two votes to sixteen.

Incidentally, in the bar there is a notice on the wall. No TREATING, No LADIES, EVEN ACCOMPANIED BY GENTS— with three exclamation marks after that. Just behind the beer hatch is the medical dispensary. The hospital is full of contrasts like that. You ignore them, just as no one ever asks the question why a certain patient is there, or what happened to him before he came.

Sometimes you can guess, without asking, that it is the question of a malaise of the spirit. Many of the fighter pilots there are suffering from what is medically known as nerve stress, a collapse from having been driven too hard, too long. Now there is an ever-increasing influx of new pilots into the Service, squadrons can be rested in turn and more often ; but there remains the aftermath ; the men who, when I used to stay with them at their Stations, called their uniforms their sleeping suits because they were never out of them, standing-to day and night, to take the air at five minutes' notice, and challenge overwhelming odds.

When they first come to the hospital, not surprisingly, they cannot bear the sound of a telephone ringing ; they are so certain it must have a message for them. They cannot sit in the same room for more than five minutes. They cannot read a book. They can do nothing except think of their squadron, their friends, put out their hands, even in their sleep, to touch the cockpit of their machine.

And then little by little, their overwhelming sense of exhaustion and inertia leaves them. But what is most difficult of all to cure, and why for so long they will not mix with their fellow-patients, is a sense of guilt, even though so often they wear a D.F.C. ribbon on their chest. Yet they still feel, utterly wrongly, that they have let down their comrades because they have to be out of the fight for a time.

That is a very dangerous neurosis that has got to be fought and discarded and destroyed, not only in the R.A.F. hospitals but in every ordinary community. For, as the C.O. explained to me : it is something which all of us may have to face before the war is over. The truth that some people possess greater powers of nervous resistance than others, and if they crack, you should not blame them, only seek to help them, remembering always that it may well be your own turn next.

As for the scars that lie upon the surface, next time you or I are complaining because we are stiff and aching from a chill, you might remember, as I shall remember, going into the gymnasium of this hospital, and looking at all the special appliances designed to help men whose bodies are encased in plaster, whose hands have been burned and bent and made powerless, aiding them little by little to get back the power to hold out their hand once again to life.

And look at that dartboard in the corner. Next time you play a game in your favourite pub, think of these fellows who at first have to take up their stand only a foot away from the board, because they cannot reach any further, because in fact, they can scarcely bring their arm up to their shoulder at all. But they persevere, until in the end, they can throw again as pretty a dart as any one.

The man who helps them is someone I have known for a long time and respected and admired. His name is Dan Maskell. In the old days, I used to watch him patiently coaching our Davis Cup team, surrendering his own pleasure in the game, his own personality, to aid their confidence, and especially the superiority complex of the young ladies, who because they had reached the centre court, used to give themselves the airs of film stars.

Now his magnificent fitness, his ability to place a ball on any foot of the court, is serving a new and greater purpose. What about knocking up with me for half an hour? What about a game of squash? he suggests. The patient shakes his head. He is still too inert. He cannot bear the thought of a game, any kind of game, and then somehow, the flickering spark which has never quite died, rekindles. He hears that the boy in the next bed to him succeeded in standing for half an hour with a squash racquet in his hand and he knows that he is in plaster from shoulder to waist. Well, if he can do it, he thinks, even if I cannot use my right hand or the right side of my body, what about trying with my left.

And so he goes on to the court and Dan feeds him, and the first few days there is hardly a rally. And then in the end he is asking Dan to remodel his backhand, just like one of the rising Wimbledon stars—but with this difference. He does not want it right for Wimbledon, he merely wants to fill in the time before he gets back to operational flying.

And he goes back. That is the point. The hospital is a home for two hundred men at a time; at an average, thirty are coming in and going out every week. And it is true that not all of them can ever be fit to again fly, say, over Germany. But that does not mean that their usefulness to their country is at an end. Many of them go forth as instructors, to be regarded henceforth as heroes by their pupils. And justly so.

One of them dined with me on Boxing night, in a hotel not far away. Another grand hotel, not commandeered for the war, but still full of rich men and women, who can afford to be expensive refugees in a comparatively safe seaside town. This boy watched them dancing round. He watched them ordering champagne. He watched them put the paper caps on their heads. I watched them, too, though most of the time, I was watching him.

There was no bitterness in his gaze, even though ever since the war began, he has been in a night-flying squadron, and you can guess what the strain of that is like. But he did say something which I think should be repeated. He said : Sometimes, when I see Churchill's speech quoted, about the many who owe so much to so few, I wonder what will happen to us all after the war. I sometimes feel that we shall be the many then, out of a job, and it will only be the few who will remember. . . .

Do not misunderstand me. The men in this hospital I visited are very grateful to that particular hotel who have done much to entertain them. But for my own part, the onlooker who records all that he has seen everywhere he goes, I cannot help thinking that there is still too little equality of sacrifice between the different communities of this country.

Outside that one hotel, the cars rolled up for the Christmas festivities. There seemed to be petrol galore ; certainly there was money galore. Outside the other hotel that is now a hospital, there stood the hotel bus and the C.O. happened to say how he wished there was a bit more in the patients' entertainment fund, so that he could afford to run that bus to take the boys for trips. He did not add, as he might have done : That bus *must* be run, the boys have a right to such trips.

That contrast stays in my mind, and others, too. At the corner of the road, going down into the town, one day, a patient stood waiting for the bus. Dan Maskell gave him a lift coming by in his car. He could see that his hands had been terribly burned, and he broke a hospital rule to ask what had happened. And his companion said : " Well, my machine caught on fire, but I did not want to bale out until I got the other fellow, it seemed a pity, so I had to wait a few minutes."

That was all he said.

That evening, there was a concert in the hospital, and the star attraction was four fellows dressed up as Westerners, singing hilly-billy choruses. And then the moment came for one of them to sing a solo, the leader turned and said : Now, our first hospital V.C., F/Lt. James B. Nicolson, is going to oblige.

The news had come through that morning and that morning as usual F/Lt. Nicolson waited for the bus, and was delighted to get a lift, and still he dismissed his own story as just one incident in the Air Force tradition. That tradition which was defined for me by one of the doctors in the hospital, who is very close to the men he loves to serve. He said : The three outstanding qualities they possess, is a sense of reality, a sense of simplicity, and a sense of generosity. Just as they never shoot a line themselves, so they cannot be deceived by any kind of line of talk from other people. But sincerity of any sort they recognize and accept, even though the other person may have nothing in common with themselves. There lies their generosity.

As for their simplicity, you only had to watch them undoing their stocking and exclaiming over each item, a pair of black service socks, a tube of toothpaste, a packet of cigarettes. . . . And as for their sense of reality, he added : " If the war achieves nothing else, it does at last make us all obtain a right perspective about what is worthwhile and what is not. It gives all of us a chance to find ourselves. And to these men here in my care, even when they are in the vale of darkness and unable for the moment to look into the light, I try to explain how, just as a new year wipes out the past year, so does every new day bring new opportunities for happiness. They are children, wandering in the darkness when they come here. But we are all children, all pilgrims searching to find the same road, home."

And when I had finished writing down what he had said, I found that the night had gone and I was no longer alone in the train and another journey was at an end.

Chapter Eight

A DAY OUT IN DEVON

You may be looking at the title of this chapter and thinking it out of place against a background of Air Force blue. But there is a connection ; a rather important one ; and a link, too, with the previous chapter. I hope you have not forgotten already what I said there about the hotel bus which stood empty in the courtyard because there was not sufficient money to run it. Don't feel guilty, there is no need. All I want to explain is that since I wrote that last chapter and it first appeared in print, contributions have come in from all over the country which I have been able to pass on to the C.O. of the hospital. In consequence, the bus *does* run now and will go on running I hope and believe until the end of the war. That is not a hint. It is just a fact.

When I paid my next visit to the hospital, the winter had gone, Father Christmas had put away his red cloak in moth balls for another year. And in the courtyard, an almond-tree was in blossom, frail and transparent against the stone of the wall. It was the first flowering I had seen and I looked at it and then at the resurrected hotel bus waiting to take us for our day out over the moors.

You had to admit, all the same, it was a heavy morning. There was no sun, and when I saw my companions, many of them with the scars of battle upon them, for a moment, despite the almond-trees, I could not believe that the spring was just over the hill. Packing in was difficult, too, because so many of the fellows had their legs in splints, and had to have room to stretch and a safe place for their carpet slippers. Some of them, I noticed, had brought shooting sticks, as though we were off to a Point-to-Point, and one of them wore a tweed jacket and cap to match, such as in peace-time you used to see so often at the races. His Blenheim fighter had run out of petrol, and he was lucky really, to be there in the bus at all, setting out on one of the expeditions which the bus does every week now.

As we took the high road, three cars fell in behind us. " You see, we've got a fighter escort," said one of the pilots in my row, with an accent which I rightly guessed to be Canadian. Nearly every one had brought a map of the country with him, and there was a good deal of chaffing about that when, in Newton Abbot, we took the wrong road, and I suggested how odd it was that after all their training in map-reading in the air, they should not be able to find the road to Widecombe.

Every one laughed at that, except the Polish pilot, who just went on looking at the map. I suppose he did not understand, or perhaps he was thinking of his own country and what the map would be like when the war was over at last. I never heard him speak the whole journey.

It was market day in Newton Abbot. The little town was crowded with carts and there were open-air stalls, and at one of them two pretty girls with scarves round their hair were picking over the stuffs, pondering no doubt which they would choose for a flowering summer dress. Every one looked out of the window at them, as at a view, and lit cigarettes.

At last we were free of the battle of the carts, and the Canadian said that the rich red earth reminded him of his home, Prince Edward Island, and his next-door neighbour replied : " I thought you came from Canada." To which he retorted : " But Prince Edward Island is the smallest province of Canada." I nodded myself, not knowing a bit about it really, but thinking secretly how strange it was that when the war happened, we were so ready to make a fuss and welcome to service men from our Dominions, but in peace-time so few of us took the trouble to find out anything about their country.

And so we came to Ashburton and on to Widecombe. As the hills became more switchback every mile, someone muttered that it was like dive-bombing, still too near to the other thing to free his mind completely. But I suppose that was inevitable, because when, in one particularly narrow lane, the sides of the bus grazed against the hedges with a kind of swishing sound, I heard an exclamation : " Ah, shrapnel." And from three or four rows in front of me a whisper, almost as though you were dreaming it, added : " But, oh boy, where's the flak ? "

The day was beginning to lift, the soft Devon rain had ceased, and our spirits had lifted, too, when we reached Widecombe at last, and it was still just the same as it had always been, with the shop on the left where you can get the pottery, and next to it the inn, and opposite, the Church House, and by the Green the sign depicting Uncle Tom Cobley and all.

Like every one else having a day out on the moors we went first to the inn, and afterwards to see the Church House. In the inn, we all had cider. Pints of it. " Rough or sweet ? " the barman asked us, and we all voted for sweet. The Canadian had some, too, though he assured us that he was permanently on the wagon, and we assured him in turn that it was not intoxicating, and he believed us.

There we were, clanny little groups filling the two parlours, and somebody said : " Now, what about some bread and cheese ? " and a chorus went up : " Have you forgotten, old boy, there's a war on ? " All the same, it was rather surprising not getting any cheese, because it was a day when we were all trying very hard not to think about the war. Indeed, one of the pilots with the D.F.C. ribbon on his tunic, introduced me to his dog, and the dog was a Cocker spaniel puppy only five weeks old, and I had a sudden longing for my own dog, Mr. Sponge, whom I have hardly seen since the war began. But you cannot get away from the war even in a Devonshire pub, for on

Next time you come across a fellow with one wing upon his tunic and an O beside it, shake his hand and offer him a drink.

the walls was the map which shows the Ruhr and all the industrial centres which we were bombing with ever-increasing force.

I suddenly sensed that the boy next to me was not listening to the conversation any longer about the respective merits of cider and beer, but was staring, rigid and silent, over my shoulder at the wall. And then I remembered that, before his Blenheim crashed, bombing the Ruhr had been his nightly picnic. And I remembered, too, how at a station from which I was myself flying, they showed me the photographs of Hamm before we blitzed it and afterwards. Personally, I wish that every one could see those photographs, because then we would all understand better why you at one time heard the word Hamm, Hamm, Hamm on the radio until it became a kind of joke—except to the men who do the job.

I wish, too, you could see all the snapshots I took of us having our picnic high up on the moors near Leusdon. Perhaps once upon a time long ago you took the same road out of Widecombe and had the same crisis when you reached Ponsworthy Bridge. " Talk about so much being owed to so few," exclaimed one fighter pilot. " This is the real problem, of how can so much get through so small a space." But in the end, we scraped through, and piled out on to the side of the road and the unpacking started and the cry went up, " Grub, grub, grub."

There was one cardboard box full of hard-boiled eggs done up in bits of newspaper. It was a long time since I had had a hard-boiled egg, and it had never tasted so good before. We picked off the paper and the shells and scattered them over the grass, and someone said : " Aren't we being rather trippery ? " And the answer was : " Anyway, it's better than scattering bombs." He meant, of course, enemy bombs.

High above our heads a buzzard came into view. And one of the bomber pilots suggested, a little wistfully, I thought : " How lucky to be a buzzard—because then, without even using your wings, indeed, by no apparent means of support, you can gain height instead of losing it at crucial moments." Another fellow assured us it was all a question of thermal currents. I knew nothing about that, but I did know that every moment it was getting warmer, not only the sun coming full out, but also the atmosphere was changing, and feeling that my companions, incarcerated for so long because of their honourable wounds, were subconsciously being revitalised by their day out on the moors.

After the picnic a vote was taken as to the rest of our itinerary, and complete unanimity was established at once. They wanted to go to Princetown to see the prison. I suppose to reassure themselves how fortunate they were to be alive, and free men.

On the way, we stopped at Dartmeet, where the two rivers join in a sunlit, dancing melody over the rocks. And some of us were content to stand idly on the bridge and throw pebbles, and others went off by themselves, exploring along the banks. One boy, I noticed, wherever we stopped, went off by himself at once. And I shall often see him in my mind, hurrying back, dot-and-carry-one, at the last moment, so as not to miss the bus.

There were a good many challenges here about crossing the river stone-hopping, instead of hedge-hopping for a change. I issued one myself. " Go on, Stan, you won't get right down to the bridge without falling in." And he started off at once with his groggy knee and all, and because of that fell in with one foot up to his knee. Afterwards, as he dried himself on the bank, enjoying the joke as much as any one else, he said it reminded him of an occasion once in New Zealand, when for a charity show he drove his motorbike right off the pier into the sea. That exhibition had been child's play to him, really, because you see, the air gunner drying his foot was Stan Greatrex, I suppose the most famous speedway rider who has ever packed the stadium at New Cross in days of peace.

So we went on to have a look at the prison, and now the sun pouring into the bus made us all sleepy, and heads began to nod, and it was good to see them sleeping, with no nightmares and aided by no sleeping draught, but simply through fresh air and sun, and a feeling of freedom. And then we came to the prison and every one woke up, and I got the same feeling in the pit of my stomach as I always do, when I see the tiny gratings instead of windows.

We came back another way through Totnes, and once we had to stop because it smelt as though our brakes were on fire, and it was funny in a way to see the concern of those who, in the air, never hesitate to take fantastic risks, getting all het-up over a brake drum being hot. But really I think it was an excuse to linger at Holne Bridge, where again the Hurricane pilot walked off slowly by himself. When he came back and climbed in he volunteered : " I think I shall have to take up fishing in my old age. I see now how pleasant it must be to have an excuse to sit by a river for hours."

In Totnes we all had tea. They did their best for us at the hotel, but apparently the others did better at the milk bar. When our half-hour was up we compared notes, and it was just like a school treat, the grub we'd eaten still looming as the most important object on the horizon. The boy in the tweed cap was munching a wafer ice.

All the same, it was not like going back to school really, because when we finally reached the hospital there was no evening " prep." In the courtyard I ran into a patient I had not seen since my visit at Christmas. I described him in the last chapter, you may remember, as a second Bader. Well, he was going to have a party that evening to celebrate, for he had just heard that he had been passed by the Board for flying duties once more. His crutches were gone for ever, he was going to take the wings of the morning again.

So I gave the bus a pat on its buttocks, where it had grazed itself against the Devonshire hedges, and I suddenly noticed that the almond-tree looked twice as bright and twice as springlike as it had done when we set out . . . was it only a few hours before ?

Chapter Nine

DRESS REHEARSAL

You are under arrest, he said, as I came up the steps of the Station Commander's H.Q. Before I could ask what for, he added : You're in the enemy's hands. We are the " enemy."

For one wild, woolly moment, I thought this was the invasion at last, and that my German captor had pinched the R.A.F. uniform with the wings upon its tunic that he was wearing. And the next second, I had recognized him as a friend I had made in France in the early days of the war. How's your baby ? I asked, for his daughter created a kind of world record by travelling to America on the Clipper when she was three weeks old, and never crying once during the whole journey. Swell, said John, and went on with the attack.

Some of the attackers had discovered a way, on paper, they boasted, of reaching the nerve centre of the Station. But for all their schoolboyish relish on insisting that they had captured the telephone exchange, the exercise was in deadly earnest. If the Germans do try to land on any of our airfields . . . well, let them try.

This Station, where I was just arriving to spend a few days, is the headquarters of the School of Army Co-operation. While I was there, I saw the whole " works." I was allowed to fly four times on different patrols that the Air Force carry out with the maximum of efficiency to provide the Army with eyes in the sky ; on a low recon-naissance, on a live shoot, on a sortie at night, and on yet another tactical reconnaissance which took nearly two hours, when the enemy, having landed on our shores, were supposed to have advanced some considerable distance, and we had to discover what concentration of troops or material there was in a certain area.

Half-way through this last trip, our machine suddenly

gave a stomach-heaving lurch, as a fighter skidded past us on the left, and I thought : It's happened again. My pilot had the same idea. He shouted cheerfully, a moment later : I thought we were being attacked. It turned out to be a Hurricane, who proceeded to formate on our machine, so close to us that he reminded me of a puppy dog wanting to be noticed.

My pilot grinned at that simile when I suggested it to him later on the ground. I wish I were in fighters, he said. So many pilots who fly heavy machines express that longing, and yet, if the invasion becomes the reality which I am assured at every Army or Air Force headquarters I visit, it is bound to be in the end, then A.C. squadrons are going to play as dangerous and vital a part in the defence of our country, as they are performing on the Middle East Front at this moment.

Yet the truth is, that up to this time, the hundreds of pilots who had been trained for this type of work, have received little limelight and less recognition. But just think for a moment of their training. It has been likened to a machinist in a factory, suddenly confronted with the job of working four dials at once and sweeping the floor at the same time with a brush held between his teeth. For the A.C. pilot has to be able to take photographs, pin-point an area within a hundred yards, receive and send back Morse, drop bombs, do artillery and tactical reconnaissance, have a working knowledge of the Army, *and* fly the machine.

But the actual flying is the last thing we are concerned with, they told me. We are a floating platform for observation. Perhaps you still think that sounds simple enough. Maybe it was—in peace-time. But what about the squadron of Battles, who in the first winter of the war, went over the Siegfried Line and hovered there, the murdered prey of the flak, while they took their photographs at 3,000 feet.

Now we have made such great strides in photography, that we can by the use of infra-red films and using a long-focus lens, procure equally good photographs at 30,000 feet. A new technique has emerged. But the glory of past exploits remains, and I think it is only fair that one day, the story of that Battle squadron should be told.

As for the future, it was very heartening to have the privilege to hear some of the secret discussions in regard to new theories, new technique, and at the same time, have the chance of talking to the pilots themselves, many of whom are veterans from the Battle of France and the Battle of Britain.

Come into the hangars of C Flight with me. You know, that flight-lieutenant wearing the D.F.C. on his tunic, who is kindly helping me on with my parachute gear, is *very*, very lucky to be alive. He won't tell you the story, but I am sure he won't mind my doing so.

On one occasion, his Lysander in France was attacked by no less than nine ME. 109's, of which he succeeded in shooting down two, and taking successful evasive action against the other seven. When you consider that a Lysander has been likened to a bus because it has to be as steady as a bus for taking photographs, and is hopelessly unequal to aerobatics—or weaving, as they call it in the Service—then you can realize just what a feat that was.

On his next trip, he was not so lucky. Shot down over the River Dyle in Belgium, the next thing he remembers is waking up a month later in an English hospital. To this day, he has no idea how he got there. He has one vague recurring dream, which is of being bombed in the ship which brought him home. And yet another casualty on that same crossing will tell you that the ship had a peaceful passage. But one thing emerges from all the surmise. He *is* alive, and thrilled to be back in harness again.

My own pilot on the live gun shoot sortie also wore a ribbon on his tunic. I imagine I am right in stating that he is the only pilot in the British Air Force to wear that long, red ribbon. Very embarrassing, he says, because it is so like the V.C. and people in pubs are always mistaking it for that. Actually, not so long ago, some people might have suggested it was embarrassing for another reason, for the ribbon is the French Legion of Honour. Thank heavens we are at last beginning to take a more realistic view in regard to our late Allies.

But we are in the air, and cannot talk, John and I, about the French, because he is too busy plotting the progress of the guns. It is his role to record the white puffs and send back a message by wireless as to the exact position where the shells are falling. For instance, on the ground, they get, perhaps, " B 6." B represents two hundred yards out, and 6 is taken from the analogy of a clock, to explain that the shells have fallen due South of the enemy position which is being attacked.

Sometimes, the A.C. pilot knows the target, exactly where it is on his map, before he sets out. Sometimes he has the more difficult task of finding it and giving it to the guns behind the line, ready trained to fire. I visited one of their batteries, manned by lads from the North. What's that you're munching? I asked as they stood to between shoots. Gunners' tiffin, they replied in chorus. And what's in it? That's what we're trying to find out. Still, there have been no actual deaths yet, another volunteered. I noticed that there were no sandwiches left over, however!

Our mobile light guns are very impressive, in their way as impressive as the great fixed batteries I have seen on the southern coast. Lift it up, the Commander said. *Lift it up?* I repeated. But to my astonishment, I could raise the support at the base, bringing the gun round forty-five degrees in as many seconds. The Commander explained what an advantage this meant, if tanks were advancing towards you and suddenly changed their direction.

The A.C. squadrons often have to act as Close Support. Take the question of invasion again, or the present Eastern campaigns. If the troops on the ground advance so swiftly that they get out of reach of their gun support, our planes take over and do the job for the artillery. They bomb machine-gun nests, troop concentrations, communications, anything which lies in the way of the advance.

Every Army corps to-day has aircraft attached to it.

These come under the direct control of the Army, though naturally, the C.O. of the squadron has the last decision in regard to weather conditions or the number of machines he can put into the air at a given moment.

In the mess of the Station I visited, there were many officers in khaki with wings upon their tunics. They have been seconded from their different regiments to the Air Force for four years, to be trained as pilots, so that when they return to the Army again, they will be thoroughly air-minded and consequently invaluable through their knowledge in strengthening the ties of co-ordination between the two Services. Incidentally, I have never visited an Air Force mess with so many moustaches. Another proof of the Army influence ! In the mess, too, I heard the best story yet of Teutonic thoroughness.

An officer had been dining the night before with a woman friend who had recently escaped from unoccupied France. One evening, in her hotel in the South, a German soldier, apparently very drunk, barged into a French officer with a row of ribbons across his tunic, and spat in his face.

You have no right to wear those ribbons, you ran away, he sneered. Whereupon the Frenchman knocked him down and a proper party ensued. At the height of the mêlée, two German officers appeared, and immediately, on learning what had happened, dressed down the soldier—in fluent French. A guard was summoned, and the civilian audience were assured that the offender would be put under close arrest and court-martialled in the morning.

Naturally, every one was very impressed by this display of discipline and tact, even the Englishwoman, until a day or two later, she discovered the whole thing was a frame-up ; the French officer was himself a German ; the scene had been staged and worked out and performed with perfect timing to the last detail, simply in an effort to win over local opinion. What do you think of that ?

But come along, we can't wait to swop any more yarns, now the fog over the hills is lifting sufficiently for us to do a Low Reconnaissance. Imagine yourself in the gunner's

This fair lawn, with the cedar trees and the pillared façade of the noble house behind them, was occupied until the day war broke out by the Queen of England's father.

seat, whose job on operational manœuvres is to keep his eyes glued on to the sky above. On this occasion, I was much too fascinated gazing down at the earth below. A hundred and eighty miles an hour, at twelve feet over the ground. I have never had such a sense of speed before. It is like all the dreams we have all had, of being lifted up off the ground and just floating over the treetops. Add to that the sensation that you are in a runaway express and nothing is going to stop you, and you will have some idea of what it is like.

Our job on this occasion, is to make a tip-and-run raid over enemy occupied territory, to discover whether a crucial bridge has been blown up. Look out, there are the enemy. See how they run. Poor, silly sheep, why be frightened of us ? The cows go on browsing, they do not even deign to turn their bovine heads skyward. Only the sheep take to their legs across the plain. How lucky you are, I thought, you have none of the problems to face of us human beings, in war and peace. You just munch and munch away and become mutton at the end of it, and you never guess or worry about the fate that is in store for you.

But if I envied the sub-human existence of the sheep for a moment, I felt very differently that night when I flew again, under a full moon and the lights from the flare-path transformed the landscape into a technicolour film. The dull green of the earth becomes vivid emerald, we take off and all round the sky are dotted the red and green navigation lights of other planes, practising night landings.

Soon we are sailing serenely over a sleeping city, and there beneath us is a great and noble church to which men have paid pilgrimages for more centuries than you have fingers on your hands. There are some moments when every one of us feels that the world is ours for the asking, when you are so sublimely at one with the elements, that you feel remote, apart, a god. Come invasion, come war, do your worst. This moment you cannot touch. And this was such a moment.

We are down on the earth again. Soberly my pilot and

myself walk back towards the mess. Suddenly he breaks the silence with a laugh. What's the joke? I ask. Where-upon he said : I was thinking of the story of the little evacuee who was always hearing grown-ups talk about invasion, so she made up a special prayer which went like this : Please God, bless the Army, please God, bless the Air Force, please God, bless the Navy, and please, please God, take great care of yourself, because if anything happens to You, we're sunk.

Chapter Ten

"FEAR NAUGHT" IS THEIR MOTTO

In the previous chapter, the Army and the Air Force got together in co-operation, and following that up, I feel it is only fitting that the last chapter of this section of my book should be devoted to the description of a very happy and inspiring visit I paid not long ago to a famous Army camp, where in the last few months, an innovation has come into being which is proving a triumphant success.

The innovation is a newly-formed Young Soldiers Regiment of boys between eighteen and nineteen, who too impatient to wait to be called up with their age group, feel quite rightly that there is as great an honour and satisfaction in training to be a tank commander in one of our panzer divisions of to-morrow, as in volunteering to be a bomber pilot or a rear gunner. And because of the wonderful spirit of dedication that you will find among these boys straight from school, I would like to take you with me to visit their camp. Ready?

The gritty, parching dust rises in our faces on the plateau, swept upward by the wind from the wild, un-trammelled valley, stretching away into the autumn haze, remote and geographically vague. Are we in England? Are we in Africa?

The dust is the same. The tanks are the same. The

heat of action and excitement and the exhilarating sense of a new kind of warfare, are the same. The heat engendered when you are inside one of the Valentines, the driver, for instance, holding on to the two levers which form your steering wheel, the muscles in your arms stretched taut and challenged, as you go over the top and down, down into the valley, negotiating the hostile terrain and the unknown booby traps, taking them in the slow, lumbering stride of your caterpillar track.

Around me on the plateau were a group of pupils, waiting their turn to go for a ride. Their youth is a kind of armour in itself for whatever lies ahead. For they are so very young. Not one of them more than nineteen, and they let me share their tank exercises, like a new boy may be allowed to join in a game in a school playground.

I found my Valentine easier to drive than I had expected, though I had had plenty by the time we at last got back to the ridge again, and our instructor jumped off the top and exclaimed hopefully : Still alive ? Peering out of the cubby-hole which is the driver's seat, and wiping the dust out of my eyes, I was reminded of a story I had heard in the mess the night before. This had come from a tank commander who recently had been speaking of his personal experiences at Tobruk to these young members of a Training Regiment of the Royal Armoured Corps.

One day when his tank had been out in a sortie in the desert, after seven hours he clambered down like our instructor had done, and peering in at the driver with whom wireless communication had broken down, asked : How are things, Jim ? His team-mate grinned back, his face obliterated with sand and sweat and the dust of battle, and this was his reply : Oh, things are fine with me, thanks, but oh I do wish I had my mother-in-law with me !

Things are fine, too, with these young soldiers whom I visited the other day. And I wish you had been with me to see them going full out at their course and you would have been impressed as I was with the same atmosphere of urgency and proficiency and friendliness combined, as you will meet in an R.A.F. Training Wing.

Just as a boy joins the R.A.F. with a vision before his eyes of one day being the captain of a bomber raiding Berlin, so do these youngsters of eighteen, when they put themselves forward as malleable material for future tank crews, secretly sustain themselves with the thought of the day when they will be able to say " mind my tank."

Even if that does not happen, they are consoled with the knowledge that just as the R.A.F. officially admit the equal importance of the wireless operator and the gunner on board, so is the same view taken in regard to the format of a tank crew. Thus already at this new training school is being engendered the same sense of comradeship and team spirit among the different batches of recruits as you will find with bomber crews at an Operational Station.

Moreover, the analogy goes further. A Whitley or a Stirling is just as likely to have as its captain an N.C.O. as a pilot of officer's rank. In the same way, every boy who volunteers to-day to join this Young Soldiers' Regiment knows that if he makes good in the course of his preliminary training—and that is entirely up to him—at the end of his course he will either pass on to an O.C.T.U., where he will be groomed for a commission, or, raised to the rank of an N.C.O., he will be sent for further training to a tank depot. But—and this is very important to remember—whether he eventually passes out as an officer or an N.C.O., he still possesses the same opportunity of one day being a tank commander.

And now I expect you would like to have some details of the course itself. Well, for the first few weeks, the boys have to submit to the usual training on the square. But these panzer recruits do not mind this, for three reasons. First, they know that it really is going to be weeks and not months and that there are all sorts of exciting things ahead of them. As soon as they finish with the square, they will start being shown how to drive and maintain their tanks, and then there will be weeks of gunnery and eye-training and instruction in crew control ; followed by wireless classes, and then after a week's leave, to give them a breathing space richly deserved, the course ends with collective training, when every point in the whole curriculum is put into practice in an imaginative programme, while the boys go miles afield on manoeuvres and camp with their tanks under active service conditions.

The second cause of their confidence is that they know that there are no kinds of distinctions at this school. On the square, I passed a new batch of recruits drilling and my companion casually picked out for me from the platoon, the anonymous figure of a fair, straight youth, the son of General Martell, following in his father's footsteps, and then a rank or two behind, a boy who in private life is a peer, and while I was thinking about that, thinking how this is what the word "democracy" really means, my liaison officer added : " The other day, a housemaster at Eton passed on to our C.O. the letter he had received from one of his old boys, saying : " In my hut, I sleep next to a chap who used to be a slaughterer. I am glad I sleep next to him as I like him the best of all in our hut."

And the third reason why they are so content goes deeper than the fact that their grub is first-class. I had dinner with them one day during my visit and I can vouch for that, and also that their winter quarters will be dry and warm. But what warms their spirit most of all is the positive knowledge that the right man has been put in charge of their training.

When they first arrive—each week a new batch of recruits, and still they come—their C.O. has an informal talk with them about mechanised warfare and the tank training that lies ahead of them. And spontaneously he says something which is typical of the man. With a twinkle in his friendly eyes he gives them this piece of advice : " The great thing about being in tanks is that when you are in action, there are so many things to think about that you do not have time to be frightened."

They accept that truth from him and are reassured by

it, because they have already seen on his tunic the ribbon of the M.C. which he won in action as one of the pioneer tank commanders in the Battle of the Ypres Salient. Thus the barrier between the two wars, the two generations, is bridged, and later when they come before him, individually, for an interview in regard to a possible commission, you feel that there is no barrier between his side of the desk and theirs.

I sat behind his chair in his plain office hut and on either side of the colonel were two company commanders who had put forward possible names. The dossiers lay on the table ; the boy's school ; what games he played ; what examinations he had passed. Such a dossier is necessary, of course. But at the end of the morning I was completely convinced that it was the interview itself that counted, or rather the report on the boy during his training, supported by the impression he made as an individual when he had the chance to speak up for himself.

I noticed that the colonel's first question was always invariably the same. Why do you want to be an officer ? To which one boy who came from a London secondary school replied : " I think I could serve my country better in that capacity. I am eager to have the opportunity to lead and look after my men. And I am sure that the responsibility would make me a better soldier."

It was a fair and honest answer.

Privately I recorded that of the boys who had been put forward that day for interviews by their officers, a greater proportion came from elementary and grammar than from public schools. Another thing which struck me was how many of these young volunteers came in the first place from the Midlands. And one of the officers in the room himself volunteered as the door shut behind a candidate : " We've an awful lot of fellows lately from King Edward's School, Birmingham."

As this was my home town, I was particularly interested and I knew that this school had a great reputation in the past for producing first-class Rugger sides. Of course, the physical side of training to be a member of a tank crew is of paramount importance. So these boys are encouraged to play games in their off-duty hours, they go for cross-country runs, and one evening I watched them boxing in the stadium.

It was a night of novices' contests. And it was grand to see the guts they showed. It made you feel that though they may be still novices in regard to tanks, that by the time the moment comes for them to leave their training Valentines and go into the real battle, that they will not let down the workers who on another front are sweating with every sinew now to double and redouble the output of tanks.

The day after I said good-bye to this Young Soldiers' Regiment, I had an engagement at Port Sunlight (the first and still the best of the garden-city-cum-factory-layout) to speak to the workers there who for many months now have been having a great savings drive for tanks. I was able to bring them a message. I told them how in the wireless section of the school, I went into a classroom where a dozen recruits were taking it in turn to send out a message in morse for the others to pick up. They could choose whatever message they liked. I looked over the shoulder, by chance, of one youngster, and this is what he had written on his pad :

WHAT YOU KEEP FOR YOURSELF YOU LOSE, WHAT YOU GIVE AWAY YOU KEEP FOR EVER.

And what I shall keep for ever is my last memory, when I stood at the edge of the parade ground and watched the colonel carry out his weekly inspection of these youngsters, as tall and upstanding as guardsmen many of them, who whether they have only been there a few weeks or are just passing out from their course, have already the stamp of soldiers who have henceforth dedicated their lives.

It was early in the morning. A new day's rigorous training was commencing. The air was keen and cold and reality shone upon the scene. But as their C.O. took the salute at the march-past, you were warmed by the strains of the band playing that proud, familiar air, " My Boy·Willie."

Well, if your boy Willie has joined or is thinking of volunteering to be a member of one of the panzer divisions of to-morrow, I can assure all parents who may chance upon this book that they can confidently echo the two famous words that make up the motto of the Royal Tank Regiment : FEAR NAUGHT.

Act Three

Chapter One

THE EDGE OF THE WORLD

FROM the pinnacle of the crag where the coast road in sheer exhaustion slides sideways over the hill, I waved my hand in greeting. Far below me, silhouetted sharply against the dazzling sugar-white lighthouse buildings, I could see the foreshortened figure of my host waiting. Another adventure, like another year, was about to begin. . . .

But the last mile down took almost as long as it usually does for me to leave London and reach my country home. Still, my welcome was worth it. And you would have felt the same had you been the guest on New Year's Eve of Mr. and Mrs. Andrew McMillan, who have been married for thirty-three years and have themselves lived in half a dozen lighthouses, before they came to the Mull of Kintyre.

If you ask Mrs. McMillan which she liked best—was it Buchanness or Sule Skery or Inch Keith or Ailsa Craig—she simply smiles and says : I liked them all ; while her mind goes back across the years and her grey hair, parted in the centre, is fair again and she is remembering how, when her time had come for her first son to be born—the one who now wears the coveted letters " N.L.' in his cap like his father—they sent a pigeon with a message and it flew the ten miles to the mainland so swiftly that within half an hour the doctor was climbing into the boat. And now in the present, she adds : If you are happy as we have been, I don't think you notice the place very much. It is our hame. You and your man are together. And the days seem to pass so quickly. . . . Whereupon her husband broke in gruffly, but with a belying twinkle in his eyes, so used, so trained to see beyond the near horizon : " Sometimes in the summer visitors like to have a peep at what we

ourselves call ' the edge of the world.' They come scrambling
down the side of the hill, puffing and blowing, and then
seem quite disappointed and surprised to find that we haven't
heather in our hair. . . ."

The heather in the late summer carpeting the Mull
must be a bonny sight, too. Even to-day, in the little patch
of garden sheltered from the Atlantic by a long, white
wall, where the principal lighthouse keeper—to give him his
official title—and his two assistants in their watches off dig
for victory and grow giant cabbages, while their womenfolk
hang out their washing on the line and tend the forty fowls,
there is a veronica bush in full bloom beside the sundial,
defying the knife of the keenest Nor'-easter.

When the weather is in that direction, Mr. McMillan
sets out before sundown to walk the long mile along the
coast path up and down the steps dug out of the side of the
cliff, where somehow a few mountain sheep find both sus-
tenance and a foothold, till he reaches the foghorn on its
isolated eminence. Inside the hut, like a ritual in a church,
he lights two paraffin lamps to keep the machinery from
freezing up, to make sure that no ships will founder from
that cause. . . .

" Do you get many birds here beating their wings and
killing themselves against the light at night ? " I asked.
My host shook his head. " Ne'er a one ! " And went on
to tell me how he had a letter from a learned professor,
inviting him to send off any birds that were found dead in
the morning for examination in a laboratory to explore—
a new theory this—whether they were carrying foot and
mouth disease. But I was thinking myself at that moment
of the little French poem I once heard sung in Paris by
Agnes Capri—where is she now ?—about a lighthouse
keeper who had such a deep love for birds that it became
too great an agony for him to find them in the morning
battered against his tower. So one night, he broke faith
with the mariners : to try and save his other friends he
shut off his light. When the dawn came, it was to find that
a boat instead had been battered to death against the rocks

below—a boat he later discovered, whose cargo had been one of precious humming-birds being brought from South America to an English aviary.

I was still too shy to recount this story and its moral to my host, for had he not suggested as we climbed up the steps, that there's a good old Scots saying that every time a sheep opens its mouth to bleat, it misses a bite. However, on our way back to the lighthouse proper, he did break the silence to tell me that long ago, there was another saying that when mole hills came to the Mull of Kintyre, it would mean the end of the world. Well, there were plenty of mole hills at our feet and that catastrophe was still far away. Here we were, only standing on the edge.

As for the other calamity which now muffles the heart-beat of Europe, Mr. McMillan agreed that " You wouldna' know here there was a war on," and shielded his eyes from the last of the sun as he gazed across the water at the Irish hills. So near they seemed that you could almost put out your hand and brush the bloom off them like the bloom from a grape. While away to the right, he pointed out the Paps of Jura with their first mantle of peaceful snow. I might have been standing there still, had not Georgie, the little evacuee lad from Glasgow, who swears he never wants to see the city again, but to live all his life in a light-house, come running out to tell us that tea was ready.

Won't you come inside the sitting-room with us? It is very pleasant there with the fire burning up.—Mrs. McMillan told me that she uses ten tons of coal a year provided by the Northern Commissioners—and there are the kind of home-made scones which you only get in Scotland. The talk is of Hogmanay and how fortunate it is one of the lighthouse assistants is as dark as a Spaniard— I nearly said Italian—so that he can play the part of " first-footer " at midnight and cross the threshold with a piece of coal, some flour and a bottle in his hand, to represent food, warmth and drink in plenty for the coming year. And I suggest that the bottle had better be my flask, which last time came in useful to greet the New Year on the bridge of the minesweeper, the *Polly Johnson*, whose guest I was out on patrol, for surely the toast we all drank that night brought us luck during the year. For though the ship went down at Dunkirk, were not its crew saved ?

My hostess smiles at my simpleness as she pours out another cup of tea and looks at the clock, though here they live by the sun and not by the artifices of summertime but by the unchanging lighthouse law which decrees that at every dusk, the lamp shall be lit and stay bright until daylight puts it out once more.

Mr. McMillan has two assistants and David Rendall, the learner, who take it in turn to keep three-hour watches during the night. When there is a fog, they stay on duty for six hours at a stretch. They must not read a book nor write letters to while away the time. Perhaps that is why the bookcase of leather volumes in the sitting-room contains only bound editions of *Good Words*, *Welcome Guest* and *Leisure Hour*, dated 1865, 1860 and 1857. The only anachronism in their midst, if you like to call it so, is a scarlet cloth edition of four Edgar Wallace novels strung together. Still, my host admitted that he liked a good adventure story and would welcome some new volumes to add to the lighthouse library.

Soon it is blackout time. How strange it is to hear the familiar words, to watch the familiar precaution being carried out here in a lighthouse, where the nearest policeman is nearly twenty miles away and where any chink of careless light must be blotted out a hundred times over by the dazzlin radiance of the lamp now revolving in the tower room overhead, a lamp which possessed 281,000 candle power.

Let's go up the spiral stairs and have a look at it in its setting of polished wood and spotlessly-kept brasswork. Something I have always wanted to do. Something I have wondered about so often when I have seen the light from the water. I had imagined a great electric globe like some colossal chandelier and instead—you may not believe me for a moment, but it's true—the actual lamp itself on its pinnacle is no larger than three ordinary gas mantles put together. Indeed, it looks just like a nursery gas mantle whose globe has been left off.

David Rendall, the learner, is on watch and he explains to me that the lamp uses five gills of paraffin every hour. The foundation revolves on a basin of mercury and that's why, I suppose, the structure is so silent, so effortless, so altogether supernatural somehow. Below is the clockwork mechanism which has to be wound up every half an hour when a bell strikes to warn the watchkeeper not to let the machine run down. At first, you feel that a three-hour watch must be an unconscionable long time with so little positive action. And then little by little, the love of the lighthouse keeper for his lamp takes possession of you, too. You are caught up and suspended in the beauty of the polished reflecting prisms of heavy glass, which literally multiply the light a thousand times and which, as you stand on the upper and outer wooden platform, give you the impression of a great, inimitable cavern of glittering mirrors stretching away to eternity. One moment, in your eagerness to reach even closer, you crawl through one of the gaps on to the revolving platform itself—it revolves completely once a minute and the light flashes every thirty seconds— and now you go so close to the flame that it is scorching your cheek. So you back away once more on to the outer stationary platform and turn away your head and put your hands like blinkers beside your eyes, to keep out the light and press your cheek against the cool glass of the tower's globe itself and now beyond there is another world, the world of the stars and the moon and infinite space.

The boy at your side, in his soft sing-song voice, is telling you how he comes from the Orkneys and how he never left the Isles till he came to train as a lighthouse keeper. He is very proud that he was chosen from many applications and there are few vacancies in this band of under three hundred men all told.

Among other qualifications, you have to be twenty-four and unmarried at the start and have a trade like a mason or a blacksmith : David tells me, too, how he does not smoke nor drink and how two Hogmanays ago, a bottle of whisky was passed round at midnight, but he refused it, and how the next spring, when the ploughing competitions were being held, there were more bottles for prizes. With his strong arms, this great fellow with the fair head of a Norseman won the first prize and the prize in his case was a bottle of lavender water. He smiles at the joke at his expense. He can afford to smile. He is a man. A man who knows what he seeks from life ; a human being who is completely content with his lot on earth. His teacher has done nigh on forty years service as a lighthouse keeper. David Rendall looks forward to a similar dedication, an equal test of solitude, a mate—he showed me her smiling picture carried always in his pocket-book—as kind and gentle and single-hearted as Andrew McMillan's lady.

To have been their guest, even for a brief while, was a wonderful experience. When midnight came, my host tramped up the stairs to relieve the learner. For a moment, we were all there on the platform together and my flask passing from hand to hand. Yes, even the learner's, too, just for luck. And as I go forth on further adventures, I shall often in my mind's eye see them standing there on the narrow ledge of the lamp's platform, poised as it were between one year and the other, between one way of living and the other way, too. The clean, ungreedy, clear-cut life of these two men, representing two generations, too, and the grasping never-satisfied bauble-seeking existence of so many of us, represented by that great glittering globe of light and its thousand prisms.

But Andrew turned his back on it and peered out to sea. He was thinking of the men whom he helps to guard and like Captain Miles of my minesweeper a year before,[1] unconsciously echoed the same New Year resolution. " A man can only do his best in his job from day to day, and not worry. That's never got any of us anywhere yet. Don't worry," he repeated.

[1] See Godfrey Winn's *On going to the Wars*.

And the rolling of his r's, like a beat of drums, reverberated round that tower, multiplied like the light, reaching —or was it only my imagination—far out beyond the curtain of glass to all the men who look upon a lighthouse as their friend, reaching out to all of us who are friends this day in a common cause.

Chapter Two

ST. DUNSTAN'S LOOKS FORWARD

I CAME over the Clee Hills down into the valley beyond. Behind me lay the completion of a speaking tour in the Midlands for the Ministry of Information. For once I would have liked to idle away the promise of the morning, for this country was imprinted deeply on my childhood's memory. Perhaps because of the years between, perhaps because of the time we have been at war now, I saw it all, and the sweep away to the Welsh mountains in the distance, with new eyes.

And yet, perhaps, there was really another reason why I took off my sun-glasses and gazed so deeply upon the view. Ahead of me lay yet another rendezvous. And at that moment I was dreading it. I am ashamed now looking back, but it is difficult sometimes to assess the noble immensity of ordinary human beings to suffer and increase their stature and in the end emerge triumphant from the blows, yes, any blows of fortune.

Over two thousand years ago, Aeschylus wrote a tragedy about a king who was blinded. The greatness of the theme sometimes makes the writer. I wish it could be so in my own case. For there is no doubt about the theme itself. All I can do is to try to recapture in simple universal language what I saw when I visited the new St. Dunstan's training centre at Church Stretton in Shropshire. One thing is certain. No tragedy lies there, either on the wide terrace at the back of the house, where in their leisure hours between their lessons in Braille, the men sit with their faces turned towards the light and the green meadows, while newcomers receive assurance from the happy voice of Mr. Anderson, the first inmate of St. Dunstan's in the last war, who sometimes spends a holiday among them ; nor on the little hill outside the front door enclosed with a wire rail, where every morning they take their exercise finding the way to self-sufficiency. So many steps to the left, so many steps to the right. So many steps to the left, so many steps to the right. Only falling back on the wire guide as a last resort when we are lost, they said to me smilingly.

Nor again in the hospital attached to the grounds, where every ward is full of flowers and the patients ask their nurses to describe the flowers, the foxgloves that have no scent except in the memory of those who were country-bred. Like the boy who came back to life but slowly, staring for many long days in silence up at the ceiling that he would never see again and then, at last, he broke his silence to the nurse who leant over him. "*I am so glad that I shall have the opportunity now to take up the profession I've always had a hankering for.*"

This boy wanted to be trained as a masseur. They are all trained to be something, to be able to earn their living again in open competition, to be beholden to no man. It is the rock on which the whole structure of St. Dunstan's training is founded. To send them forth again knowing that they can pull their weight once more as citizens of their country and thus to obliterate pity. Self-pity most of all. So as to help them build up a self-protective armour, their teachers, every member of the organization, deliberately refrain from open sympathy. They control their voices. They hold back their hands from rushing instinctively to a pupil's aid every time he stumbles. And when they speak of the circumstances when " so and so got his packet," they lay no more emphasis upon the words than if they were referring to a superficial flesh wound quickly mended.

Everything points forward. The atmosphere of optimism at first seems exaggerated, almost unreal. Then, little by

Above) " You wouldna know here there was a war on," Mr. McMillan said as he gazed across the water at the Irish hills.

Below) In the garden of the Mull of Kintyre Lighthouse, where they grow giant cabbages and hang out their washing on the line.

little, you came to realize that the patients are the real people, you the blind shadow.

There is Andre, much loved in the community, who " got his packet " at Dunkirk, and talks of the day when he will " see " Paris again. There is Mr. Russell, wounded at Arras, who before the war used to work for Leeds Corporation, and by the time this appears in print, will be back at work again for his old employers. There is Jan Losowski, who in performing prodigies of valour in Norway had his sight blasted for ever.

Jan is making a box for his captain. He stands very upright beside the bench. I can't think of anything to say to him for a moment, because I am remembering what someone has told me, how, when the day came for him to go to Scotland to receive the Polish equivalent of the V.C. from the hands of General Sikorski, he confided in his teacher thus and thus : I shan't come back, he said, because when I come among my Polish comrades again they will let me march shoulder to shoulder with them. No one will notice that I am blind. To the stranger standing beside his bench, he said : After the war, when I get back to my country, I shall send a big present of wood of Polish oak to St. Dunstan's.

And then he started to whistle as he went on with his planing. It is my most lasting impression. I suppose I shall never hear an errand boy whistling in the street as I write without remembering the way those others whistled, a kind of secret morse code on which they all fell back whenever they felt they were losing their grip for a moment. They could not find the gap in the doorway, or put their hands on a tool, or the Braille lesson wouldn't go right. Then instinctively you saw their lips starting to purse, framing, as it were, their own " S.O.S." to themselves. And then the next instant, the notes coming forth. . . . Normal, unhurried, gay . . . and their confidence is instantly restored.

Someone who helps their confidence greatly is Mr. Burman, who shows you the basket his pupils have made and explains how, when their course is at an end, they will be set up by St. Dunstan's in their own workshop near to their own home and be enabled to obtain materials at a discount. And it is only when he adds how important it is to be patient at first and not worry because your hands won't do all that you ask of them that you realize that the man speaking to you who moves so easily about the room has himself been blind these twenty years.

"I tell them," Mr. Burman said, "that I was just as clumsy and slow as they are once. It all comes easy in the end if you just stick at it." "And what do they talk about while they serve their apprenticeship under you?" I asked. My companion chuckled. "What do men talk about all the world over? Girls, of course. . . ."

I found it difficult to return his smile for a moment or remember how many of them were married and what a success those marriages still are until I met Mr. Preedy in the part of the school given up to training telephone operators. The blanks that were once his eyes were turned away from me as he concentrated on the earphones over his head. I could only see the curve of his freshly-shaved chin, his curly black hair, with the brilliantine shining on it, his hands darting all over the switchboard and never faltering as his teacher went through yet another dummy drill.

"The B.B.C. have just come through," she said. "They want to speak to the matron. Will you see if she is in her room? If not, go on trying to find her. . . ." Mr. Preedy got his packet at the Albert Canal. In peace-time he was an engineer. It is his last week at the Centre before he starts his new job working on equal terms and pay with the other operators at the switchboard in a Government office. The hundred mark in such operators has just been passed. That is a red-letter day for St. Dunstan's. On another machine, Mr. Preedy was tapping out a dictated telegram in Braille shorthand. I watched him, fascinated. His precision, his accuracy as he translated the message back aloud. And after ten years I can still only tap out on my own typewriter with two fingers, I thought.

I was made conscious of that comparison again when I came back to the main building and found in the library a fair lad typing away as fast as my secretary. Yet they told me that he has only been blind for a few months, a legacy from one of the last blitzes on London. His name is " Bill " Cowing. He was a member of the Plumstead Home Guard. And he is seventeen. As I stood at his shoulder I could not help seeing the first sentence that he had written before I realized it was a letter. He had written : " They say I am getting very brown . . ."

He started to fold the piece of paper methodically and put it in the envelope and then stick it down, and then he made for the door but could not find the handle.

I was just about to move forward, but my companion took my arm. The boy stood very straight with his hand out in front of him. He must have been as conscious of us as we were of him. And then he started to whistle, and in the gap which was like a century before he found the door-knob at last, I was thinking of another letter written at that same desk on that same typewriter. A boy was writing home telling his mother how he went for rides on a tandem cycle with one of his teachers, and how he had bathed (she turns her back while I undress) ; and how they had a dance every week, and had got up a play and the local audience could not believe that the actors were blind, they never stumbled once. (The trick was different thicknesses of mats for them to walk about the stage on.) And how they played dominoes with raised figures. (The winner of each round took the " kitty " of a halfpenny.) . . . " And I've put on nearly two stone in weight. . . ."

Then he folded his letter as methodically as I had seen " Bill " Cowing fold his with my own eyes, but when his mother received it, it was only a blank sheet of paper. You see, he had never known—how could he know—that someone had forgotten to put in a ribbon.

Well, I can only hope that what I have written here in this chapter may have helped a little to fill in the gaps. . . .

Chapter Three

NIGHT SHIFT

THE SNOW is falling steadily. You cannot see it, because there is no light to see it by, except that one small, dim blue lamp over the gateway, but you can feel it against your face as you stand there beside the Home Guard sergeant and listen to the shifts, like ships in the night, passing each other on their way in and out of the factory. It is half-past nine on a winter's evening somewhere in the Midlands.

Mind moi bike. . . . What's in " snap " ? Turkey. . . . TURKEY. . . . Joe's got turkey in " snap " . . . The joke about what Joe has brought for his supper rockets down the line and away into the hinterland of the Black Country, as the night-shift pile into the clocking-in hut and take their cards out of the rack. Men and women side by side, and their cards are stamped with the same letter. P. That letter stands for " PROGRESS." A symbol it was for me of the new turn the war has taken, but for the men with concrete minds and concentrated purpose, who manage this factory, it means one thing and one only. It means two million anti-aircraft shells produced since the war. The two millionth that very day.

I watched the girls taking off their coats. No fur coats yet like the last war. No shawls over their heads, either. Sometimes they have wound a scarf round their hair, more often a snood of the same material as their coat, copy of a film star's outfit, and the face underneath no less pretty. When they get inside the " shop," the brilliant mercury vapour lamps, stretching at intervals down the thousand-foot ceiling, will turn their make-up purple, their powder green. But they still wear their make-up as part of their working uniform.

Sometimes a face looks different already. Its owner went through the last war. Worked in a munitions factory then. Never believed that she would work in one again twenty-five years later, and in trousers. All the women wear trousers, even the ones who are very broad in the beam. The men make jokes about that, but not about their work. The woman are too good at their work for jokes. And when the raids come, they do not even lift their heads from the machines.

Look at that girl over there—we're inside the "shop" now—working at a grinding machine, with two girls watching her. I congratulate you, Nancy Perry. Such a short time ago you had a job in a grocery store and you threw it up because you got sick of customers asking you why they could not get more than one tin of this, more than a pound of that. You were a manageress, but because of what you felt for your country, you were willing to start all over again as a trainee and you trained so well, that already you are helping the newcomers. The sparks from the machine fly up into your face and you pay no attention, you wear a protective mask of stiff gauze over your eyes and nose, like a smart woman's veil. But your hands are filthy. How do you clean them? I ask. Oh, just soap and water, you reply. I notice that your nails are still varnished. Behind you, there's a great, grizzled fellow looking on and helping, too. An ex-boxing champion who defeated Phil Scott on one occasion, Phil Sales, invalided out of the R.A.F. because of his heart. But still of use to his country.

Still of great use to their country. Look at them, right the way down the "shop." Men of fifty; men of sixty; some day the story of their return, to themselves a miracle, to munition managers a god-send, will be told. The men who came back. The men who thought they were on the scrapheap of industry and are now getting their chance again as the young 'uns are called up, and holding their job down like a young 'un, so that their particular bench never holds up the pace of each billet of steel on its way from one end of the shop to the other, going through no less than thirty-five processes in all before it finally becomes a shell-case, polished and perfected.

And now look at the younger ones who go into action

every shift. The de-scalers, the squeezers, the furnacemen. Let's go back to the beginning, to the far end of the forge where the billets of steel, cut into lengths several inches long, are fed into the furnaces whose flames make them red-hot, even to twelve hundred degrees centigrade, whose flames lick outwards between the cracks in the doors, with an energy only equalled by that of the men as they labour, the heat of their determination to keep going, to keep going.

Words, you may say? All right, here are facts. On the night of the great Coventry raid, this particular factory, well into the battlefield, had its highest output of any night-shift since the war began. That was their answer.

The hours spent in the shelters are nil because the spotter system works, though it's mighty cold keeping guard up there on the ridge which overlooks the forest of the Black Country, the forest of chimneys now obliterated by the black-out and not sending forth a single spark between them.

I remember so well when I was a boy in this country, how the reflected glow of the furnaces used to give me a free Guy Fawkes show every night from my nursery window. It is like coming back in a dream, out there in the lonely stillness of the snowy night. And for the spotter at my side who keeps guard through the long night watch, whose home is still here? It must seem stranger even than a dream to him . . . how he must miss the familiar landmarks by night . . . how he must long sometimes for the warmth of the furnaces, the comradeship of his mates, who wear towels round their throats to keep the sweat from running down their chests.

I was grateful to get back to the heat again. I could have stood for the rest of the night watching the billets come out of the furnace, watching the de-scalers with their six-foot long " bulldoggers " fasten on to the sizzling, embryo shells and handle them as delicately as a hostess will lift a precious lump of sugar on to the end of a pair of Queen Anne tongs.

Forty-five times the process is repeated and then the furnace has to be re-fed. And after a time, the energy of the men too. Two o'clock. Break for " snap." Has four hours of the shift gone already ? I have watched the billet which sheds about a third of its weight in the processing, pierced, put on a forging machine, go down the conveyor, be short-blasted, centred, rough-turned. . . .

All right. I am not going right through the thirty-five processes. I stuck myself and the reason I stuck at the rough-turning machines and could not have enough of their beautiful precision, watching the six in a row, was not because I know anything about machinery, but because I knew that they had come to us by courtesy of the enemy. These machines were bought in Germany before the war and I should like to think that some neutral newspaper will quote from this chapter, if only to tell the Germans that our scientists have succeeded in improving the efficiency and speed of these machines a hundred per cent ! Incidentally, the King paused a long time in front of them, too, when he visited this factory. And smiled as you would have smiled.

Joe is eating his " snap." Not the Joe who has brought turkey sandwiches, but another Joe. He wears a faded blue jacket, he looks like a figure out of " Petrouschka " ; all his life he has been a basket-maker and now no one wants his baskets any more, and so he is an oiler in the factory. He helps to keep the machines going, the machines that are greedy for " snap," too, for they never stop for twenty-four hours of every day and night, though they are completely overhauled every fifteen weeks. The same system works as with the men. There are eight for every seven, which means that every one of them carries on for seven days and then has a complete day off.

I came across one fellow in that factory who particularly appreciates that day of freedom. How did he put it to me ? Sometimes I have an itch in my foot to be off again and hold my thumb down. His thumb down on a golf club, he meant. For I was talking to Frank Little, who for ten years was high up in the professional golfing world in the States. When I asked him who was the greatest golfer he had ever seen, he replied instantly : Walter Hagan, and added in explanation : You see, he had the true measure of greatness, always to have the power somewhere inside you, however much you seem to be kidding on the surface, to produce the right shot at the right moment.

Joe is eating his "snap" and talking to me about books. I like Carlyle's *French Revolution*, he said, but not so much as the book I am reading now. What's that ? I ask. "Gibbon's *Decline and Fall of the Roman Empire*."

Nearby, a group are playing nap, dealing the cards as swiftly as West-end club players, lest they miss a single hand. Their half-hour break is so quickly over. They only pause to swill down great gulps of tea from their billy-cans. Tea that is so strong, so thick, you could stand a spoon up in it. How do you manage now for tea ? Oh, we manage, they said. And what about sugar ? I persisted. Oh, I have the old woman's sugar. And what does the old woman do ? Oh, she goes without. . . .

Now they are scrambling back to their machines. They can go on smoking, though, if they like. One fellow told me that he used up two packets of Woodbines on night-shift, but three if he were on one of the day-shifts. In rotation, the men work on the three shifts ; six in the morning till two in the afternoon, two till ten, ten till six.

At four o'clock, I left them to it, wishing that my experiences of that night could have been shared by all the other soldiers—are not these men in the factories soldiers, too—for whom these shells are specifically made. Just as many of our fighter-pilots have been visiting Spitfire factories, would it not be possible for some of our Ack-Ack gunners to have a day off themselves in an armaments works and see their shells in the moulding, and best of all, swop yarns with the men who make them ? I believe that would have wonderful repercussions. So many of us these days carry on with our war-work blindly, our nose so near to the common

(*Above*) He has an ordinary sort of name—Fred Brown—but no ordinary sort of job.

(*Below*) Frank Willis wears no uniform. He didn't even wear an overcoat on the journey, nor carry a tin hat.

grindstone, that we never pause to lift our head to get the thrill of the final climax, the encouragement of the ultimate result.

Instead . . . like blind fish we are. No, that's not my phrase. As I came out of the dazzling blue-lit " shop," I stumbled in the sudden exaggerated darkness and someone took my arm. An old man whose shoulders were powdered with snow. What was he doing out there in the cold? Let him speak for himself. " *Gaffer, what would they do without me? Like blind fishes they are . . . and I lead them.*"

Even as he leads us across to the other building, plainly now you can hear the sound of a truck being emptied on to the swarf heaps. The swarf which is the turnings from the steel and which will be used again. That is the old man's job, to wait outside and help the men from stumbling in the dark. That is his cog in the machine and he is content.

Upstairs in the directors' boardroom, someone has put up two camp-beds. One for my guide, one for myself. And I think of all the other offices now in war-time, where men sleep beside their desks. In a couple of hours, you will hear the shift going off, my companion tells me. They make quite a din, usually, he added.

I did not hear them. And the last thing I remember is gazing at the two shells, set out like sports trophies, on the table beside my bed. The one which was the first millionth, and the one added to it that day, the second millionth. How many more millions will be needed? It is a profitless question. Better to turn over the page, and embark upon a new chapter, a new adventure on the home front.

Chapter Four

NIGHT EXPRESS

No ONE notices him as he goes down the platform in the black-out, patiently making his way through the passengers catching the down train to Windsor. In the darkness, they cannot see his blue eyes that from long years of service as a motorman can see in the darkness, his sturdy, shortish figure, his dark blue tin helmet set square on his grey hair. They are all too busy with their own preoccupations, listening to the reverberating gunfire overhead, the magnified drone of the planes which seem unpleasantly near to the glass roof, wondering how and what time they will reach home.

I had never noticed him before last night, either. But I shall never travel in war or peace at night again, without thinking of the driver whom I want you to meet, too. He has an ordinary sort of name, a typically British name—Fred Brown—but no ordinary sort of job, as I discovered when I travelled beside him in his cabin at the front of the train, that tiny, barren space eight foot by five, unheated, unfurnished, which for over ten years now has dominated his working life.

Suddenly, as we wait our signal to be away, we see what the passengers never see. Like the lights, announcing the star's name outside a theatre, straight ahead of us in the darkness go up two large shielded letters. W T. That means Windsor on the through line as opposed to the local line. We are off.

Once upon a time Fred Brown drove his train at nights at forty, fifty miles an hour along a floodlit track, with nothing to combat except fog and rain clouding his lookout window. Now he takes her—trains, like ships, are feminine to the men who coax them—at a steady fifteen, and when I asked him how he knew he was going fifteen, he simply replied that he did know, although there is no gauge, no way of proving his instinct right.

During the journey, Fred Brown paid a spontaneous tribute to his comrades and especially to the signalmen who have to stay put all night in their boxes, suspended there like giant pigeon lofts, though with scarcely the same cooing accompaniment to the work which goes on inside. I understood, because the previous evening I had spent several hours in one of the largest signal boxes in the Metropolitan area, where there are no less than three hundred and eleven levers controlling track points and where over two thousand trains pass through every day. Twelve years ago, it took the place of seven signal boxes at the cost of over £200,000. Not long ago, all the miraculous scientific devices which go to its make up were nearly destroyed, and much more besides. A bomb of the heaviest and most unpleasant kind struck the roof a glancing blow and slid down on to the track. Whereupon three men, wearing no uniform, in their shirt sleeves, gave each other a swift glance and then turned their eyes back to the great diagram board in front of them, with all the track points illuminated upon it indicating what trains were coming in and out of the station and where they all were at that moment. As long as that board went on functioning, the various tiny globes spaced out along the chart, going black to show that a train was occupying that section of the line and then white again to show that it had successfully passed on—they themselves would go on functioning, too. And these are the names of those three men, because I think their names deserve to be recorded, just as much as the names of so many other heroes on the civilian front to-day. Tom Hulbert from Peckham Rye, who has been a signalman for twenty years, Harry Lewis from Camberwell, with even longer service behind him, and Ernest Baldock, who lives at Forest Hill and plays the bass drum in the station orchestra.

Tom Hulbert was rolling a cigarette when I talked to him. It was he who in a moment's respite from his duties, decided to go down the wooden steps and have a look.

Someone said to him in the darkness : It's a bit of an aeroplane. So Tom Hulbert went up and touched it. " It's still warm," he said, " but that's no aeroplane." Then he went back up the wooden steps, back to his mates. It was an hour before they received an urgent telephone message to evacuate their box. " But we brought all our trains in first," they told me in chorus, with affection and pride.

Incidentally, the station-master, in the course of coping with the flap that night, did something he has been warning passengers about for many years. He stepped plumb on the electric live rail—but like the bomb, by some miracle, did not explode either !

Every signal box, every bridge, every large building, Fred Brown, the motorman, knows by heart, every level-crossing has a memory for him—" that's where Jerry dropped one on the line, just as we'd gone through the gates," he said—and one of the level-crossings had a memory for me, too. As we glided on in the ghostly moonlight, I saw the ghost of a small boy on his bicycle racing to get through the gates before they closed, carrying proudly in one hand a war-time prize of twenty-five years ago. The prize was a pot of marmalade which had been wheedled out of the grocer, the kid was myself.

It might have been twenty-five years instead of twenty-five minutes that I spent in the train's driving-cabin, before we drew up at our first stop, Hounslow, dead level against the tiny lamp put at the end of the platform to guide us in. The sense of isolation had been tremendous, you could not even hear how the blitz was progressing, any more than on the occasion when the Hudson I was in was shot up over Stavanger, could we hear the riposte of the enemy machine-guns. All there was in the world was the silhouette of Fred Brown, his controls, his signals ahead, green, red and more often yellow, to warn us that there was danger ahead.

Once upon a time, too, Fred Brown drove a steam engine, and when he changed over to the electric railway, at first he missed his mate, the fireman, very much. You must feel even lonelier now sometimes, I suggested. And in the darkness came back an unexpected answer. It's a treat to be alone sometimes, he said.

So leaving him there to his loneliness, I bolted back down the platform to finish the rest of my journey in the guard's van. They had warned me, "we still only stop twenty seconds at every station," and the train was over a hundred yards long. I arrived panting to hear a voice booming out the name of the station in the darkness, in a soft Dorset burr, because the guard, Mr. Wesley B. James, who after forty-three years' service was due to retire next year, pace Hitler, comes from Poole and started life as a railway boy at Wimbourne.

Now he is one of the senior councillors of the Wimbledon Borough Council and a J.P. for Surrey, and capable of dealing with any situation. A soldier was saying to him as I came up : " Where does this train go, chum . . . ? " and Mr. James, who looks like a bishop, was replying : " It's not a case of where it goes, it's where *you* want to go. . . ." Fortunately, the soldier wanted to go to Windsor, unlike one of his comrades who a few weeks ago, came up to this patriarch among guards on the Southampton express to Waterloo and threw himself on his mercy. " I am told this train does not stop at Basingstoke," he said, " and I'm being married there to-day ; I've got forty-eight hours special leave and . . ."

It was all right. The train did stop there. The boy was married, and all the superintendent said to Mr. James was : " Well, it's your fault if the marriage is a failure. . . ."

As we talked, my host pointed out landmarks, like the Feltham marshalling yards, as we slipped past a host of trucks, their tarpaulins silvered by the frost and moonlight. I nodded. Until the other day, I must confess I never troubled to look twice at such an inanimate panorama, but I feel differently now, very differently, since my own visit to Feltham and what I learned about humps.

Up to then, I only thought there were two kinds of

humps. The camel's hump and the hump we all get in war-time sometimes, but now I have seen the hump of a marshal-ling yard, where a special engine pushes the trucks up to the pinnacle and then at the signal of a shout from below in the darkness—a cry of No. 5, No. 9, No. 15, according to what is chalked up on every truck—the signalman in the box, Maurice Lockyear, sends them on their way down the incline, to any one of nineteen different sidings, according to their ultimate destination. And as the trucks disappear again into the night, there is a special gang of boys who put on the brake and prevent them piling up at the bottom, clinging like agile monkeys to their sides. When the Duke of Kent visited these yards, he specifically asked to meet the men who carry on even when the gunfire is directly overhead and bombs are dropping nearby.

These men work anything up to twelve hours a day, and only have one day off in three weeks now, and they are passing through an average of 21,000 trucks a week, and how-ever dark the night or however bad the blitz, they tell you with pride that they have never failed to pass through less than fourteen goods trains containing seventy trucks apiece.

These are facts. Dull facts, if you like. I don't find them so. To me, they are dramatic and important and historical. Anyway, there is not time to argue. Mr. James has waved his lamp. We are moving on again.

Now a fog is creeping up the line, muffling the beat of the barrage. In the guard's van, from my inglenook seat with its carpet covering and its spy-hole through which I can catch a glimpse of the line ahead, the signals are becoming dimmer and dimmer. Mr. James said : " I may have to delve into my black bag at any moment."

I had often wondered what was in a guard's black bag which looks so like a doctor's. He showed me a dozen flat red objects which look rather like red seals. I had not the least idea what they were until he explained that they were fog detonators, and if things get very bad it's the guard's job to go out on to the line, both forward and back and place one at a quarter of a mile from where the train has come to a standstill, one at half a mile, and three ten yards apart at three-quarters of a mile. " Of course, nowadays we use them more for other circumstances than fogs," Mr. James said, with the same degree of understatement which makes A.R.P. personnel refer to their night work as so many " incidents."

When we reached Windsor at last, the fog had encroached upon the platform and it was more difficult than ever to notice the figure of Fred Brown as he climbed out of his cabin and slipped away to stretch his back and legs before the return journey. I caught him outside the station yard. I wanted to wish him luck and express my admiration, but I did not quite know how to put it into words. So I said : ' Your wife must be very proud of you." " Oh, I expect she thinks I'm a bit of a nuisance—like Jerry," he replied, jerking his tin hat back off his forehead.

And now I could see that his square figure was silhouetted against the misty, immemorial walls of Windsor Castle and that is how I shall always think of him, against that background, and all the other railwaymen who perform unspectacular jobs like his, but together contribute so much to the united effort which will ensure that over Windsor Castle, a British flag will always fly.

That is a fact, too. Do you find it dull ?

Chapter Five

THEY DRIVE BY NIGHT

THIS is the story of a journey through the night, and my companion on that journey, who drove his twelve-ton lorry for eleven hours from the east side of London to Leeds City Square, where he deposited me and shook my hand and said good-bye.

His name is Frank Willis. He's a Bradford man. He

wore no uniform. He didn't even wear an overcoat on the journey, nor carry a tin hat. " You get used to it," he said. But I can tell you quite honestly that it was the coldest and, in a way, the most nervy trip that I have made since the war. Yes, even colder than in a minesweeper.

But let's start at the beginning, as you always should with a story. In a London depot all the twelve-feet high lorries are drawn up in a row, being loaded, mostly like ours, with a cargo of essential foodstuffs. Under the mercury vapour lights the faces of the drivers already look as grey as the dawn they will meet at their journey's end. Among the fleet are two going to Bournemouth, two to Southampton, and another two to Sheffield, Norwich and Nottingham ; while four are booked for Liverpool and seven will take the trunk road to Manchester.

The doors of the lorries are open at the back, up against the loading bank. Up north they refer to it as the dock, and in the Midlands as the deck. It is mostly girls who are carrying the huge packages and packing them in, so as not to lose an ounce of space. The fellow at my side exclaims with a chuckle : " You've never heard such an improvement in the language of our men since the girls started working for us."

All that matters to me is that they are very efficient and do their job. How much do they get ? Fifty bob. And the men drivers ? About five guineas. For that they drive five nights of the week. Yes, *through anything*.

I soon saw what he meant by that emphasis. As we came out in the yard another raid had started and there was a sudden crescendo in the barrage close to us. So close that beyond the open gates the whole of the walls of the buildings opposite were lit up as brilliantly as though arc lamps were trained upon them.

Already the vibration and the din from the running engines were so embracing that you could not hear how near the bombs themselves were dropping. My companion got out again and I wondered what he had forgotten. He had gone to adjust the headlamp.

St. Thomas's Hospital in peacetime. Out of this present set-back, what may rise Phœnix-like from the ashes?

" The engineers have been at it to-day," he explained, " and it's a bit too bright."

With the light opposite I thought that well, kind of funny. But I didn't say so and my companion made no comment at all during the journey about the fireworks that from time to time lessened the darkness of the road.

When the lorries have a trailer behind, the driver carries a mate, but the fellows on the twelve and fifteen-ton lorries never have a companion, though nowadays they try to give a lift whenever they can to any one in uniform stranded on the road.

" All the same, some of the soldiers hardly say thank you," Frank told me, " and I had one the other night," he went on, " who after a mile asked to be put down again. He said that my cab was too slow for him."

Actually, it surprised me very much what a sense of speed you achieve at twenty miles an hour ; much more than in an aeroplane at two hundred. I suppose it is the intense vibration that gives this effect. As the night wore on I began to wonder how Frank drove at any pace at all.

And yet, as we advanced through wall after wall of darkness, he seemed to know exactly what was there ahead and what was coming round the bend. You trusted him absolutely and you could feel the weight of the cargo giving a little from side to side as we crossed the camber of the road, and you could understand at last why lorries do not always seem to pull back to their own side as quickly as you would like sometimes.

I noticed that he never used his horn once the whole journey through, nor his single headlamp either, except at a blind corner to show that we were on our way round, or when we passed another lorry going in the same direction.

Then the procedure is like this. You flip your lamp to show that you are coming up behind. The lorry in front answers with his to show that he knows you are there. You then draw out and as you go ahead of him you continue to drive on the right side of the road for a hundred yards or so until you get another flip from his front lamp to reassure you that it is safe now to draw back in front of him on to the left side of the road again.

Our first stop was at the café three miles beyond Stevenage, which is the Savoy Grill to lorry drivers at night. It would take us an hour and three-quarters to get there, Frank said. No express train in peace-time could have been more punctual. At exactly a quarter-past nine we drew up, arriving there via Stamford Hill, Wood Green and the North Circular Road through Barnet. Once as we came up to a roundabout, Frank had jerked his head and explained : " The lorries which are going to Birmingham, Manchester and Liverpool carry straight on here." " What's it called ? " " Bignall's Corner, South Mimms." As we swung away ourselves to the right, I thought : At this corner the drivers make their bow to destiny. It may well be that their journey to the Midlands will coincide with a blitz, while their comrades going further north will escape. And then another night . . .

Well, we provided the postscript to that ourselves, because later we were to hear that twenty minutes after passing through a certain town, a stick of bombs were dropped on the very road where we would have been had we lingered another twenty minutes at Jack's Hill, Graveley.

Here Frank had a bacon sandwich and a cup of tea, and I had some sausages—two helpings because they were so good. I was glad to stand up and eat and stretch myself, though I would have liked to have got nearer the fire, but already there was a crowd encircling it. A little boy of ten leant against the knee of one of the drivers. And there was one girl only, in a clean white overall. She was laughing and joking, but there were none of the lorry-jumping dames that you used to hear a great deal about in the old days, pestering the drivers.

Frank said that the war had quite cleaned them off the road and he told me a story of how one night a few years back—he's been driving for thirteen years—he came out of a café and found a heavy-weight blonde curled up in his seat. " Where do we go from here, luv," she greeted him. She went exactly four feet into the roadway.

Frank, at thirty-seven, is married and has two boys, one of fourteen and one of ten. The elder boy, Kenneth, has just left school and is apprenticed to be an electrician. His father thinks that is a fine trade for him, and I agree. The boy himself is mad keen to become an air cadet and train to be a fitter. They live with their mother at No. 15 Anvil Street, Morningham, Bradford.

" In Bradford we pay 11s. 6d. a week rent, whereas when we lived in London for four years we couldn't get anything under 25s. a week. And none of our neighbours would talk to us then," Frank added. I am always hearing that criticism of that unfriendliness of the south. Is it just ? I'm afraid it is.

Anyway, they were friendly enough on the road that night. There was " Lofty," for instance, who, when our engine wouldn't start, came to the rescue, standing on the handle while Frank swung. I don't know his other name, or I'd tell it you. Frank didn't either, though they had been meeting night after night for years.

" Lofty " takes his seven-ton lorry up to Stamford and back every night. " But one night a week," he said, " I have a gala. I go right on to York. It varies the monotony. . . ."

I suppose that's one way of looking at it. As we set off he shouted after me : " You'll know when you reach Baldock because there's a bump just before you come round the corner. When it's too dark to see anything I can still get round by that bump. . . ."

I didn't notice the bump because I was too busy trying to carry on a conversation above the din. " Ever been to Baghdad ? " Frank shouted just outside Grantham, as we came down Spittlegate Hill. I think I understand why he asked me then, because the drivers going north hate that hill most of all. It is so easy to lose control there and have your six wheels skidding all over the place.

When you get through Grantham and out the other side, the drivers regard that as a kind of milestone, they believe the worst of their journey is over and their spirits soar, so that Frank was back in Baghdad, in the army, a lad of twenty, carefree, with rupees in his pocket to burn.

And yet I don't know . . . because when I asked him what had made him become a lorry driver when he came out of the Army, he replied at once : " I always fancied the life. Here in my cab I feel in my glory."

At our second stop, our only other stop during the night, Frank left the engine running, though we stayed inside the café nearly an hour. Two miles from Newark it was, and when we came to it there was no place left for us in the parking ground, so many other lorries dark and sombre with their secret cargoes were there before us.

It was good to get into the warmth. Our cab had no glass in the side windows, but two cloth blinds like a railway carriage, which Frank pulled down. But the cold seeped up through the boards and the cracks. And not only the cold. When we came into the light, I looked at Frank and he looked at me, and he said : " You're almost as black as me." Where did all the dirt come from ? All the other blackamoors in the café looked at us, too, and grinned, while " Old Bill " behind the counter says with a great show of crustiness, " No eggs."

All the same, it was quite obvious that he hated letting down his customers, and he volunteered how he used to cook seventy dozen eggs a week in his night café, once upon a time. Frank had chips and peas and I had a rasher of bacon and some very sweet coffee. It was so warming it might have been brandy.

We stayed here longer. I could see that Frank was very tired ; he leant back in his chair and just sat with his feet up to the fire, steaming. There was one of those machines that play gramophone records when you place a dime in the slot. Unfortunately, it was out of order, because I looked at the list, written out in pencil, and they were very enticing. There was " I Cried For You "—Bing Crosby—and " Ah, Sweet Mystery of Life," " Harbour Lights " and " Sail Along, Silver Moon," sung also by Bing Crosby.

But perhaps it was as well that the machine was out of order, because at that moment a great fellow with huge alleys running down his face shoved threepence down on the counter—twopence for a cup of tea and the other penny for two aspirins. They do a roaring trade in aspirins. There are more packets piled up on the counter than cigarettes.

As we paid for our grub, I saw a notice on the wall. It read : *To avoid mistakes, will customers kindly pay on delivery*.

And I thought : I hope the other customers do, too, and realise that even to-day, thanks to men like Frank Willis, goods handed over in London in the afternoon are unloaded and redelivered in the North next morning by nine o'clock.

" Thawed out ? " asks Frank. I nod. It's a quarter-past three. We move towards the last lap. Sixty-eight miles seems much less than a hundred and ninety. But when we got to the last twenty miles of all I thought the journey would never end. I had been dozing fitfully and then I woke to see what I mistook for the moment to be a host of will-o'-the-wisp lanterns in front of us. I thought we were back on Markham Moor, where on the road near Retford Frank had had three punctures on his last journey and been stuck for eight hours, but the lanterns turned out to be bicycle lamps, the first shift of the day, though it is difficult to realise the dawn is over the hill, the darkness is too complete, and it is a long time since we have seen any traffic. Not since Stamford, when the lorries going south passed us and Frank would say, " That was one of ours, with Harry in the cab," and I'd say, " How do you know it was Harry ? " And he did just know, that was all.

We are coming into the city and the trams are starting, and Frank made his last effort to shout above the engine and the rattling : " It's a good city, Leeds, for trams. At this hour in the morning you can go for two miles for a halfpenny." Which was generous, I thought, of a Bradford man, though I was really too numb now to think of anything coherently at all.

As he draws up in the City Square the sudden stillness is wonderful, and then I discover that I am too stiff even to fall out on my side, so Frank gets down and gives me a hand, and as he uses his torch I suddenly see his face, and it is the face of an old man.

Chapter Six

HOW LONG WILL THE CLOCK STAND AT HALF-PAST EIGHT?

How LONG will the clock stand at half-past eight ? In the ghostly silence of the night, the light of a torch flickering across the wall, I suddenly caught sight of an electric clock, built into a cornice of an operating theatre still standing high up within the dangerous, derelict territory, a clock which must have stopped at the very second when the last of four heavy-calibre bombs fell plumb upon the military objective, which was a hospital.

So that now there was only the silence repeating my question. The silence which must remain until the war is over and the rebuilding of St. Thomas's can commence. But the life of the hospital still goes on. Still goes on like the ticking of a clock.

None of St. Thomas's above the ground surface is any longer in commission ; a million and a half pounds worth of damage has been done, apart altogether from the irreparable destruction of instruments, but nevertheless there is something which cannot be brutalized or beaten into submission. And that is the determination of a hallowed institution such

as this, dedicated and sublimated by centuries of struggle—
and to the folk who live in humble alleys on the southern
side of the river, this hospital in their midst has been as long
as they can remember a source of pilgrimage like a cathedral
—to carry on their work of assisting the sick, yea if need be,
even in the catacombs beneath the earth.

Once these catacombs were the storehouses. A great
passage, four hundred yards long, stretches there beneath the
earth, lit by green-shaded lamps, like a gangway in the
bowels of a battleship. Here was the laundry, and what is
the laundry now ? The new operating theatre, where
four surgery cases can be dealt with at once. On the night
when the final and worst attack was made upon St. Thomas's,
when the bomb fell through the doctors' Common Room,
killing two of the House surgeons who were having a
game of darts, and crashed down, down, immobilizing
everything, the lights, the water supply, the gas, everything,
they were just about to operate in that theatre upon a
policeman with a burst appendix.

Yet when you talk to the Sister who was on duty in
the theatre that night, she speaks of her experience, as once
in peace-time one might discuss the temporary discomfiture
of burst pipes after a giant frost. With a deprecatory smile,
she tells the story of a man who put on a pair of rubber
boots and waded about the river in the corridor outside,
eagerly taking orders from any one who chose to give them,
and it was not until long afterwards that they discovered
that this blackamoor among many blackamoors—the
dispensary caught fire and all the chemicals went up in a
great blaze—was Sir Maurice Cassidy, the hospital senior
physician, and of course one of the King's doctors.

But from that engulfing darkness there sprang light
again. A symbol, and symbols are important these days, is
that within two hours of that hopeless confusion, thanks to
lamps generating their own lights from batteries in the form
of car accumulators, yet another emergency operating
theatre was rigged up and a policeman's life was saved.
Since then, as many as thirty operations have been performed

in a day, and on nights when the attack has been particularly fierce, surgeons have carried on until the dawn, unconscious of anything except their impersonal passion for salvaging human beings, using the latest technique of surgery, which employs analine dyes for burns, and powdered M and B dressings for splints, and limbs put in plaster for months on end, undisturbed by fresh dressings, to prevent the infection, the gangrene which occurred in the last war, through too frequent exposure to the air.

(Incidentally, from burns resulting from the new kind of explosive incendiary bomb, one dram of salt to a pint of warm water will concoct a saline in which to rest your arms and hands and thus obtain some measure of relief until professional medical aid is forthcoming.)

Down there in the catacombs, I saw the trays with their instruments laid out ready for such an emergency, and the casualty ward on the other side of the passage, which they have nicknamed Scutari. And don't you think it is a fitting name, the Matron suggested, rightfully conscious of its air of scrupulous asceptic cleanliness, triumphing over every kind of architectural constriction, so typical, as Matron went on, of what the Crimean wards must have been like. So that almost you could see the shadow of Florence Nightingale walking there, whose carriage in its museum case stands as yet another symbol in the passage outside.

Improvisation, that is the real test for a tradition; smoothness, eternal smooth-running so often leads to smugness. That was in my mind when I visited the two wards, one for men, one for women, which can take seventy cases instead of the seven hundred which once St. Thomas's housed. But I was assured that though at Godalming, St. Thomas's have now opened a war-time emergency hospital with four hundred beds, whatever happens, the mother hospital intends to remain a refuge for those whose needs are too urgent to permit the journey. For instance, in the men's ward, the night I visited it, there were several members of the Metropolitan Police Force.

Of course, one always thinks of policemen being impervious to any threat. You pass them on point duty, you appeal to them in a blitz, and it never enters your own consciousness that beneath their Olympian uniform there could be any tremor of fear or pain. I leant over the bed of one of them in the Nuffield ward, and asked him what twenty years in the service had taught him about human nature. He grinned and replied : "The customer is always wrong."

The charming, grey-haired woman, head of the Lady Almoner's department, had a different story to tell ; she spoke of St. Thomas's neighbours, poor and humble and obscure, who for years have looked upon the hospital as the rock upon which their health was founded. They knew that they could go there and never be turned away. And now, in a long procession, they have been coming back, not because they are sick, but because *their* hospital has been so cruelly hit. And they come, not to ask, but to give. Old folk with nothing between themselves and the river except the old-age pension, grasp the Lady Almoner's hand, and when she unclasps it again, she discovers that they have pressed a shilling into it, without a word, for the Rebuilding Fund.

And the Lady Almoner reminded me that always hospitals have been in the front line, battling to save life, to minimize the ravages of poverty and malnutrition, ignorance, misuse. And she said with her sweet smile, like that of a nun : It is uplifting for me to sit here and listen to the stories, because however tragic their cases may seem to be, never once do you hear them complain. They accept their lot, just as the hospital itself accepts its rôle to-day.

Ever since it was founded a thousand years ago, St. Thomas's Hospital has had to stand up to the buffetings of Lear, and in withstanding the tempest has found its soul, of which even a stranger cannot help being conscious, in its shrouded catacombs to-day. It was burnt down in 1207, it was shut down in 1538, during a general suppression of the monasteries—Edward VI. later restored its Charter—and in 1862 when the South Eastern Railway decided to run a new line through the hospital grounds, the result was St. Thomas's left its old site and reopened on the Albert Embankment. Out of that apparent setback, there came the great concourse of new buildings. Out of this present setback, what may rise Phœnix-like from the ashes?

Meanwhile, improvisation triumphs. Yes, even to the construction of an oxygen tent out of an outsize Players cigarette carton for a tiny baby, while in the alcoves, where once upon a time the masseuses used to study the anatomy of a skeleton in a glass case, the cupboard is full of children's toys like a shop window. And as we tiptoed out, a kiddie with a flushed face, who has been saved from the blitz, is sleeping the just sleep of the innocent.

The innocent . . . in the women's ward, between the two rows of beds, is another cot, and in it a child whimpering, a piteous cry to heaven, for almost since birth this little boy, with a halo of fair curls, has been attacked by a desperate and malignant disease. Why should that happen to a child who has done no wrong?

It is the question which has never been answered yet. And now into it is merged the other question mark of why, why, a hospital whose only purpose in life has been to help, should be so monstrously attacked. It does no good to think like that. Come with me into the pleasant, friendly hall, still standing, where every one has their midday meal together. Watch them walking up to the counter and asking for their plate. The doctors in their white professional overalls, the nurses in their beautiful frilled white caps that look like tiaras. And then behind, the " Pinkies," named because of the pink uniform they wear, the " Pinkies " of all shapes and bulges who, for a quarter of a century, many of them, have faithfully served the floors of St. Thomas's.

On my way out, I stopped to talk to one of them. Her name is Mrs. Loder. I was impertinent enough to commiserate with her, to suggest that things must be very different now, and she picked me up at once, as sharp as you like. Different? Nothing's different, she retorted.

I was nonplussed. I remembered the moment when I

had stood overlooking the courtyard full of rubble, where amid the ruins of the dispensary, an elderly man in a white coat was searching and suddenly with a cluck of triumph, held up a bottle. Even empty bottles are valuable these days, he said. I thought, too, of the wards, all empty, the beautiful wards once full of sunlight and hope, looking out over the river and the Houses of Parliament, and then I looked back at Mrs. Loder, who with suspended knife and fork was about to enjoy her helping of boiled beef.

Nothing's different, she repeated, because the *company's* the same. And then in triumph, she gave a look round at all the other " Pinkies " who, no matter what sort of blitz they have endured during the night, never fail to turn up the next morning at the right hour.

How long will the clock stand at half-past eight ? The answer was suddenly of no importance, for here were so many manifestations of a spirit which was both timeless and of the present and therefore indestructible.

Chapter Seven

PILGRIMAGE

I DO HOPE you won't think it a bore because in this chapter I want to take you with me to yet another hospital. It would be rather strange, wouldn't it, in such a book as this, to ignore the sanctuaries where the wounded and the blitzed are made whole again. For my own part, I can only say with all sincerity that every time I drive away after such a pilgrimage, I am filled with a sense of extraordinary optimism, drunk with it, almost. And if any one who chances upon this book has any doubts as to our final victory, I cannot suggest a better tonic than that they should accompany me on a return visit I made to a hospital where once I walked through the wards and found them over-flowing with men freshly evacuated from Belgium. Now in the gardens and the grounds, here and there you meet a soldier in blue, the last of the convalescents from that first batch of wounded when the war sprang into sudden savage reality.

But in vain I looked for a face I remembered, the face of Sergeant-Major Fleming of the Cameron Highlanders who, when I asked him what it was like when the Germans attacked, drew himself up in bed, though he was in agony, and retorted in his warm, Scots voice: "What, mon, the Germans attack *us*? It was we who did the attacking!"

On many platforms up and down the country, in the months between, I have told that simple story of the faith of one man who unconsciously spoke for a whole army. And now I have another story to tell. His bed had been filled by a different sort of casualty; this great hospital in Hertfordshire has been given over to the vital work of rehabilitation for men and women, both in the Services and on the civilian front, whose primary need has been of plastic repair.

That is the phrase which the doctors use themselves for the daily miracles they perform. And when you spend an afternoon in their company and hear how, this month, they will perform their thousandth operation that will give back to some human being hope and confidence for the future, it makes you realize, had you forgotten, that miracles do still happen.

No side of medical science has taken a greater sweep forward since the last war than the branch which deals with those facial and physical injuries where a delicate and complicated system of skin grafting and complete reconstruction of bone and even nerve tissues may be necessary to save the patient's reason as well as his body.

Look at that boy of twenty lying over there on his side. Could you believe that it was only yesterday afternoon that he was flying at ten thousand feet and crashed? Use your imagination for a moment. You know what he must have looked like when they picked him out of the wreckage. Now look at his face again. Yes, it is a miracle, isn't it?

Thanks to the genius of his surgeons, his face has already been put together again, in ten days he will be convalescent, in six weeks he will look at himself in the glass, and his scars will be so negligible that he may never realize the extent of the debt he owes to those who tended him. He will fly again. He will forget.

"If only we can get them quickly enough," the famous New Zealand surgeon who was taking me round, said to me over and over again. "The time factor is so tremendously important. Even a few days can retard recovery for months. That is why we stand ready here to operate night and day on any patient. If they are too shattered to be brought to us, one of our team will go to them."

The doctors have one thought : to make it possible for their patients to go back into the world again without a sense of inferiority or a feeling of uselessness. Often, in the process of rehabilitation, a face that is being remoulded will look younger and better-looking in the end than before it was blitzed.

Sometimes, however, the doctors decide that it is not the face, but something else which is of primary importance to the victim of enemy action. They use their judgment and act accordingly. You see that elderly woman sitting up in bed talking to a visitor. She is an example of that. Her name is Mrs. Mansell. All her working life, she has been a cleaner, a cleaner of schools in Clapton.

Mrs. Mansell assured me that she felt better in herself than ever in her life. She might have added : It's the first time in my life that I've ever had a [real holiday, that I've been able to lie quietly and rest my back. And all the time as we talked, her hands, which have scrubbed and scrubbed and are now gaunt and brittle with the scars of the burning flames upon them, plucked unceasingly at the counterpane as though they could not understand their new idleness.

Those hands which have been her livelihood. Those hands which were more precious to her than a pretty face, or an unscarred appearance. The doctor beside me explained how it would take two years to clear her face of every scar. "We're not concentrating on that. She can't afford to be out of work for so long. What we are determined to do is to give her back the use of her hands."

In the next ward another pair of working hands were on view. They belonged to a fellow with a gay smile, his name was Rothwell, he has been in the A.F.S. ever since the war began, and he received his honourable scars in defending St. Paul's Cathedral. His arms were imprisoned up to the elbow in a basin filled with wax generating heat of 115 degrees Fahr., which would bring the blood back to his hands and thereby also help to bring back life and movement to his fingers. " I must get my hands right so that I can get back to the job," he said.

Then there are the hands of the pilots, who when they have been forced to bale out of their blazing machine, in the last second have had to hold on to the red-hot fuselage, while their parachute apparatus cleared itself, and in that second so often have had wicked damage done to the backs of their hands, where there is only one-eighth of an inch of skin and flesh between the outer surface and the nerve centres.

How to renew those nerve tissues and graft new muscles for those that have died. To a layman that does not seem possible. It was not possible in the last war. But they have found the solution now at the hospital I visited ; one too delicate to describe on paper, but it works.

And two other new discoveries are equally a success. They have found a way of holding together fractured and broken jaws in the period when the bones are resetting, holding them together by long, jointed pins, which are fixed through the skin from the outside and remind you instinctively of those pictures of aboriginal tribes, where the height of beauty is measured by the number of rings that pierce the lips or nose.

I was assured that these pins do not hurt the patient ; they feel no pain at all, and as a result, they are able to open their mouths normally from the very first day and eat.

The other miraculous discovery that they have made at this hospital is a formula for a new kind of jelly which is smeared over burns—the ubiquitous M and B forms part of its make-up—a jelly which reduces pain at once, prevents the wounds from festering and serves as the equivalent of a flexible rubber glove over the affected part.

In a few days the burns are completely cured. Photographs were shown to me in the clinic of a young man who looked as though he had just been rescued from the crater of Vesuvius, but your pity and sorrow is swept from your mind when you go into the ward and see the original of those pictures, for already there is not a sign to show on his pink cheeks that in the last London blitz he was on duty as a warden at C Post at Holford Square when an H.E. fell.

You would have thought there were no scars in his life at all from his friendly smile, and then he asks you to look at the snapshot propped up against the pot of flowers beside his bed. " It is my brother. He was there on duty with me. He was killed." And then he adds : " But as soon as they'll let me out of here, I want to get back to the Post. It's too quiet down here. You miss the blitz."

Those were his words and this was his name—Stan Mead. You might like to remember it.

We move on. Now we are outside, moving across the grass towards " The Lido," where officers are lying in bathing trunks, helping their treatment by sun-bathing. There is a fellow with a bandage round his head and over one eye, who looks rather as though he had an encounter yesterday with Joe Louis in the ring. When they brought him into the operating theatre, hanging on a cord below his shattered face was a message. This was the message— " *Please don't try and make me look like Clark Gable.*" When he came back to the world, it was to find that his message had been answered. Tattooed on to his chest were these words— " *Don't worry, we couldn't if we tried.*"

As we walked towards him—I noticed that the tattoo marks had now disappeared beneath sunburn—it reminded my companion of a Polish pilot, who came there for rehabilitation, but though they could patch up his face and body like new, they could not save the sight of one eye.

They had left it to the eye specialist to tell him the news. The next morning, my companion went along to his bed to see if there was anything he could do to cheer him up. But before he could even say anything, his patient with a broad grin exclaimed : " I told my left eye no good any more. I say, Good. I say, now no competition ; no mistake, with just one good eye looking along the gun. Never miss."

As for the fellow with the bandage over his eye, an Australian wing-commander, his eyesight will be all right in the end. Meanwhile, it seemed to me he saw pretty clearly with his one eye. Because this is what he said to me :

" I know nothing about politics or trade unions or all the rest of it. I only know that there is one way to win the war and another way to lose it. We've got to have more aerodromes, but wherever I've been where they were constructing one, it made me absolutely sick to see the way the workmen carried on. On one occasion, when the bus broke down which brought them to work, we sent to fetch them in one of our R.A.F. vans which is considered quite good enough to take pilots and their crews to dispersal points when they are just going off to bomb Germany, but would you believe it, those fellows refused to ride in it, they said it hadn't got soft seats like their bus. Soft seats, indeed ! I was itching to get my boot at their own seats. I wonder what would have happened to them if they had been working in Germany. Is this war a picnic or are we in earnest ? "

And the doctors standing round, who had given up great fortunes in Harley Street to serve their countrymen and women and do not count the cost, who charge nothing and ask nothing except the reward of seeing whole bodies and whole minds again, nodded their agreement for the words of truth and wisdom delivered by that young man standing there, naked except for a pair of bathing shorts, the modern equivalent of one of the prophets of old in a loin cloth.

Yes, and how long, I thought, shall such prophets continue to have to raise their voices in the wilderness ?

The "Ideal NAAFI Girl" proves that it is possible for all women war workers to be both efficient and attractive.

Chapter Eight

"SERVANTS OF THE PUBLIC"

THE LIGHTS changed, just as my car was crossing Oxford Street in the dusk, and as I waited, my eyes were caught by the poster that a newsvendor had chalked up to sell his goods. It said: RUSSIAN FRONT LATEST NEWS; and then underneath in the same size lettering: FULL AMUSEMENT GUIDE. For a moment the bitter irony of the contrast of the salesman consumed me, and I thought, as so many others must have done in the last few months: how can people go out and seek enjoyment, fill the cinemas and the theatres and the greyhound racing tracks, at a moment when this gargantuan struggle is taking place in the Russian steppes, when millions of human beings are being trampled and destroyed and blasted by the ghastly modern weapons of war? How can they . . . when every day ships are being sunk at sea . . . ships full of our countrymen fighting to keep the lifeline open to see that we do not starve? How can they . . . when every night our bombers are going off on their lonely, dangerous sorties and in the rear turret for hours on end, sits in cold, cramped confinement a young gunner, who has asked nothing from life except the chance to live, and now is compelled to withstand not only the onslaught of flak, but the nerve-racking expectation of finding himself suddenly transfixed in the blazing, pitiless sweep of the searchlights seeking their prey?

Yes, I thought like that. I compared the limelight of the searchlights, and the traditional limes of the theatre world. Artificial, unreal, tinsel light. And then the traffic lights changed and I put in my clutch and moved off across Oxford Street, and as I moved, so did my mood change. Suddenly I felt differently. The bitterness vanished. A sense of perspective took possession of me again and calmed my spirit. And I remembered other things. I remembered how, whenever I visit a Fighter Station or go out on one of my sea trips, the sole topic of conversation in the wardroom and the different messes is : What's on in town ? What show ought I to go and see on my next leave ?

And that is what the theatre does. It provides an anodyne. A blessed anodyne. A moment's respite from the reality which is the poker that stiffens all our backs to-day. And I wonder if you have ever thought of the other side of the picture : of the life of the men and women who, in this war, have somehow succeeded in keeping up the illusion on the other side of the footlights that all that glitters on the stage really is fairy gold.

You see, I know about the other side of the picture, because the theatre is in my blood. I started my life on the stage. My great-grandfather, James Rodgers, was a celebrated strolling player. My earliest memory of the theatre is being perched up in a box at the Prince of Wales Theatre, Birmingham, to see that perennial star, Dorothy Ward, in pantomime. It was the family theatre and for a long time was run by my grandparents. And now, if you walk up the street towards Five Ways, you will find that the Prince of Wales Theatre, though the façade remains, is a hopeless mass of ruins within—one more example of Hitler's accuracy in bombing military objects !

Not far from Birmingham lies another great industrial city of the Midlands—Coventry. I visited it the day after their first wholesale tragic blitz, which somehow has remained for ever after as the ultimate example of Nazi frightfulness. As I entered the city I was astonished to hear the sound of cheers, but when I drew nearer the poor, pitted Civic centre, I saw the reason why : I saw that a slim, slight figure in Army uniform was standing on the steps, acknowledging the cheers of his subjects. The King who had come to be with his people. And I walked not far behind him on his tour and every now and again, there were the explosions of time bombs going off. But he never faltered or allowed his progress to be deviated. Once, I remember, I stumbled over what I mistook to be a charred log of wood, and then my companion explained to me that it was all that was left of the body of a warden who had been known to be in a certain building and a few minutes ago had been dug out.

And so the day passed ; one of those days that stay with you all the rest of your life. At dusk, when the Royal party had left, I found myself alone for a moment in the square beside the gutted Cathedral, of whose majesty and golden canopy, wrought by the masons of the fourteenth century, Coventry's citizens were so rightly proud. All gone, all. I had stood within the ruins beside a woman silently weeping, who told me that every Sunday she had gone to give thanks there for the last thirty years, and now was bereft. Beside her was a young boy in Air Force uniform. He tried to comfort her. He said over and over again : Never mind, mum, never mind. We will avenge you. He was her son and they stood there, unmoving, with their hands clasped together.

And now I turned my back on all that sadness, as though I sensed by some instinct that there was a message for me waiting somewhere on the horizon, and suddenly above the waves of smoke and fetid fumes rising in my nostrils, a stench which I have never been able quite to obliterate since, I beheld a banner in the skies floating as though it was sustained there by the might of Heaven itself. And the banner read, in great letters six feet deep : IT ALL DEPENDS ON ME. Afterwards I discovered that the banner was on the side of Holy Trinity Church, but the smoke and the spouts of water from the fire engines obliterated the wall ; you could only see the banner, you could only remember hereafter its message.

Two months later I went back to Coventry on a Sunday afternoon. I had been asked to speak in a show organized at the Coventry Hippodrome, which unlike our family theatre in Birmingham, I am thankful to say, has escaped destruction. Of course, all the windows backstage at that time were out. It was icy cold, the troupers taking part in the concert shivered in their evening dresses before going on to the stage. I must confess I was very proud to be among them. And I was very proud of something else I was told that afternoon. Mr. Newsome, the popular manager of the theatre, had determined at once to keep his theatre open, no matter what business it might do, or what losses he might incur, but to give the town only star names—business as usual—as a gesture and a symbol of the spirit which represents the best tradition in the theatre. And that phrase " the best tradition of the theatre " can mean many things. For instance, it meant something that I had heard about by chance that afternoon. A new show was coming in to open the next day. In the cast were many chorus girls. How would they find lodgings in the town at such a time as this when so much property had been destroyed and so many of the local people were themselves homeless ? The stage doorkeeper looked at me bluntly. It did not seem to him that there was any question to be answered. Why, he replied, they'll sleep on their dressing-room floor. And I thought of the icy cold wind coming in through the shattered glass. And then I remembered what the word " trouper " really means. It means just that. No one in front when the show opened would guess that those girls had had to endure any deprivations, any difficulties, any upsets from their usual travelling routine.

Not long ago I was asked to be one of the judges to find the Ideal NAAFI Girl. Twenty-five girls had finally been selected from the twenty-eight thousand young women who to-day do such important war work serving behind canteen counters all over the British Isles, often in remote, lonely outposts. They are sometimes the only women that the soldiers and airmen see week in and week out, and in consequence, they represent something far more important than the mere purveyor of a hot cup of tea ; they represent, indeed, the ideal that every man at war carries in his heart, of the home that he is fighting to protect. And as the girls paraded in front of us on the platform in their pretty blue uniforms, I could not help thinking of that, and then I heard Lady Astor, one of my fellow-judges, holding forth as she is wont to do, about what a strong feminist she is herself, and how men have no imagination, and how all the mess that the world has got in is due to the fault of men, and how the newspapers have made such a hopeless blunder in the war in trying to glamorize the women in the Services instead of realizing that the only thing which matters to-day is efficiency. . . .

In the end I could stand it no longer and went forward to the microphone myself, although I had not meant to speak that day, and made a few, I hope, pertinent remarks. Anyway, afterwards I was supported by another member of the committee, Mr. Basil Dean, the Chairman of ENSA, who suggested that surely it was possible (whether you were considering NAAFI candidates or chorus girls or young women in other kinds of uniform) to achieve a combination of both efficiency *and* glamour. Hear, hear, I said loudly. And Hear, hear, echoed the audience, too. For, of course, that is the only sensible point of view. Does Lady Astor imagine—and I know she won't mind my pointing out her muddled reasoning, because she told me so engagingly after the contest that there was nothing she enjoyed more than a good argument—that you do not have to be efficient to get up in a canteen and sing to the workers and get your appeal over, despite the clatter of cups and saucers and knives and forks, and the conversation of the groups in the corners who prefer to play cards as soon as they have finished their grub ? And go on and do another show two hours later in another factory ; and then another show, and another ? And travel long distances under the nightmarish conditions that war-time necessitates ? And live in a suitcase for weeks on end ? And never get time to visit the hairdresser ? And still manage to look a million dollars and to have lilting gaiety in your voice and youth and sweetness in your smile and your feet as you dance ?

I can only suggest myself that you have to be mighty efficient to achieve such a continuous transformation for the benefit of men and women who are working long, grinding hours in munitions and need so vitally just such an antidote as these ENSA concerts provide. And that is why I think ENSA is doing magnificent work, and when I pay that tribute, it is meant to include not only the executive heads like Mr. Basil Dean, but also every girl and every comedian and every concert party that is now touring the length and breadth of the British Isles.

Now you will have gathered that this is a subject on which I hold very strong views because, as I have already told you, the theatre is in my blood, and every time I go into a dressing-room and sniff the grease paint, I am like an old battle-horse, scenting blood and whinnying to go into action again. Many of my greatest friends are in the theatre, and I am very proud of their friendship and I would like to speak to you about some of them now. Two names instantly come into my mind. Both of them have had those names in lights outside the theatre for many years. The first is someone who has been a *matinée* idol ever since the last war. Someone who has had more success than any one else in the world of theatre in the last decade—success as an actor, as a film star, as a writer of popular music, as a most entertaining playwright, as well as a human being in every branch of society. And still remains completely unspoilt, completely sane.

His name is Ivor Novello. When this war came, he had to make the greatest decision of his career. He had big theatrical commitments, a gala show called " The Dancing Years " which had been packing Drury Lane. Dozens of fellow-troupers depended upon him for their livelihood. What should he do ? Should he play for safety as he had every legitimate right to do ; should he plead that the war had upset everything and that he could no longer be responsible for any one else except himself ? Or should he embark upon a nerve-racking gamble and, in association with Tom Arnold, another very respected name in the theatre, take " The Dancing Years " out into the country and defy difficulties in transport, the challenge of consecutive blitzes, the thousand and one complications which make theatrical touring in war-time a sick headache for all concerned ?

Without any prompting, Ivor made up his mind. The

show must go on. It was his war job, to see that the rank and file of his profession were protected ; to see, too, that the public were not starved of entertainment and relaxation that they would need increasingly as the blitzes grew more intense and dominating. So out on tour he took that great company of over one hundred artists, and at first things did not go so well, but he never complained or gave in ; he went on believing in himself and his profession just as he went on seeing that in every town in which they arrived to perform, the chorus girls and the small-part people were placed in comfortable digs before he went himself to his hotel.

In the end success shone upon his ardour ; the tour has long since turned into a triumphant royal progress, with return dates in every big city. But what is more important, I know, to Ivor himself, is the knowledge that in this war, as in the last, he has done his job. He has proved his right to be considered one of the principal leaders of his profession. And another such leader is Jack Hylton, who more than any other impresario has been prepared to take risks in this war, to put on new shows, to keep work flowing, to create new ideas and new stars, to give the public plenty of fun and plenty of glamour, at a price which they can still afford to pay. I know him very well. And I am not shy of putting in print the fact that if I were compiling a list of the twelve men I have met in the course of my career, who have impressed me most with their sense of integrity, their grasp of what is really important to hold on to in life, and their feeling for their fellow human beings who may not always have had such good fortune as themselves, I would include the name of Jack Hylton high up on that list. And I have no doubt that others, too, who know him well, and who have themselves reached great eminence in their own world, would agree with my dictum.

For instance, I can recall vividly one night sitting in the lounge of the Midland Hotel at Manchester with Jack, when our other companion was an old and admiring friend of his—the First Lord of the Admiralty, Mr. A. V. Alexander,

As the sirens penetrated the lounge like a fog, the thread of our conversation was momentarily broken. " That is the most unmusical sound in the world to-day," said Jack, and that suggested to the First Lord a little anecdote from his youth which I think illustrates so vividly why he, another self-made man, should also not only have reached the top, but stayed there—infinitely the harder task.

" I remember," said Mr. Alexander, " when I was a kid in Bristol, earning an extra bob in my dinner-hour delivering milk cans, so that I could go to the old Colston Hall that night into the gallery to hear Paderewski play. What a treat. One of those memories that stay with you all your life. I have often spoken from the platform of the new Colston Hall and a fine hall it is, too. But my thoughts always go back to that boy in the gallery, coming face to face for the first time with genius and being bowled over by the beauty of his interpretation of Beethoven."

Jack nodded his head in agreement, for in this war, at a moment when the London Philharmonic Orchestra were in danger of having to pack up for lack of funds, he made a very brave and gallant gesture. He guaranteed them a long music-hall tour. And when all the prophets groaned and croaked, as they do at anything new, and screamed it was suicide, that music-hall audiences would never accept serious music as a change from the stories of Max Miller, Jack simply smiled and replied in his charming Lancashire voice that has never deserted him : Well, we'll see, laad.

And that was the same answer that he gave when he took Bryan Michie away from the B.B.C. and paid him a star salary and all the jealous small-timers suggested that this genial, red-haired giant who over the air had been a top-line success as a compère, would never make the grade on the road. Well, go to any music-hall where Bryan Michie and his Discoveries are to-day at the top of the bill, and appraise the reactions of the war-time audiences. It is what is in the box-office till at the end of the week that is the ultimate test. No, not quite the ultimate test. On my desk I use as a paper-weight from time to time, a long, jagged ugly-

ALICE LLOYD.

(*Left*) Alice Lloyd, a great trouper.

(*Below*) Jack Hylton, who more than any other impresario has been prepared to take risks in this war.

(*Bottom*) " Ginger " goes to Buckingham Palace with his wife.

looking piece of shrapnel. There's a story, of course, behind that souvenir, and I should like to tell it to you, and I don't think somehow you will accuse me of being a bomb-bore.

At the time when blitzes were at their worst, I was billed to make a speech from the stage of the New Theatre, Cardiff, introduced by Bryan Michie. I had just landed a w hours before from a trip in a minelayer. The trip that is described earlier in this book and appropriately called " No Time To Snatch A Harp." But I had not realized that I was going to be so much nearer Heaven or the other place that evening than on my latest sea voyage.

Just as the audience were piling in for the second house, the sirens sounded. I decided to go up on to the roof, having borrowed a tin hat from the manager of the theatre, and soon pieces of shrapnel from our own barrage fell all round me. The one that now sits on my desk actually hit my big toe. To be quite honest, it did not worry me very much, because I knew that whenever I wanted to I could go below again. But what of my companion, Fred, in his blue-and-gold uniform ? His normal job was to shepherd the audience into their seats, not to roof-spot, to take the watch, as they say at sea, and stay on. But there he was, a soldier in the front line, with nothing but a tin hat to protect him. He showed no anxiety, no emotion. Instead, he told me proudly how his nineteen-year-old son, Fred the Second, whose normal peace-time rôle was to look after customers in the Upper Circle, was signing on that Saturday and looking forward immensely to joining the Air Force.

Wouldn't you have said yourself that young Fred was already in the battle ? As the blitz grew worse, and that bumble-bee drone let forth its stings all round us, and the theatre walls began to vibrate to the sinister repercussions from the explosions, Fred the Second calmly shepherded the audience from the gallery down into the stalls. Meanwhile, just below the trap-door on to the roof were two old soldiers working the limes. It was a fantastic contrast which will stay with me all my life, to come down from the roof, ringed with enemy flares, and gaze through the hole by which the artificial rays of the limes were lighting up the antics of the actors, still carrying on. Far away on the stage beneath, they seemed in that moment to be people glimpsed through the wrong end of a telescope. Yet even at such a moment, one of the lime-men, John Stephens, who had been in the business for thirty-five years, had the courage deliberately to keep his mind off what was going on outside, and start a conversation with me instead about the great stars he had seen appear on that very stage. Vesta Tilley was the greatest of them all, he assured me.

But I could not help thinking myself that there was an equally great star on the stage at that moment. Alice Lloyd is her name ; she is the sister of Marie Lloyd, and she has come out of retirement to entertain war-time audiences in a show called " Secrets of the B.B.C." And as I gazed down at her, she was singing in a charming mauve Victorian dress, full of flounces, with a gay little parasol in her hand, one of the songs that her sister first made famous, " I'm One of the Ruins that Cromwell Knocked About a Bit." As she came to the second chorus, and gaily suggested the audience should join in, a bomb fell so near the theatre that the scenery at the back of the stage shook and began to topple, dust and plaster from the flies fell down upon Alice Lloyd's head and gathered round her feet like the shrapnel on the roof. Did she hesitate, did she even glance over her shoulder at the approaching Eumenides ? No, she was a trouper, trained in the great Tradition. The show must go on. And the show did go on until the end.

And now, except for the Epilogue, I, too, have come to the end of a drama, that I have placed in three acts, but which has, I know, many more acts to come. Meanwhile, here is one Epilogue.

EPILOGUE

THEY SAY that sequels are seldom a success. It is for you to judge whether that is true in regard to this book. But there was a sequel in my life not long ago that I cannot help feeling makes the perfect Epilogue, though, of course, again I will leave it to you to judge. This, anyway, was the sequel. I went to a war-time Investiture at Buckingham Palace, when the pilot who flew me over Norway in his Hudson on a solitary patrol, and was attacked by three Me. 109's—the full story of that trip is told in the first chapter of *On Going To The Wars*—was summoned to receive from the King's hands the Distinguished Flying Medal.

As well as sergeant-pilots and air-gunners there were a host of Navy A.B.s and petty officers, and men in Army battledress, and policemen and many Civil Defence workers receiving decorations that morning. Each one was allowed two spectators' tickets, and " Ginger " gave the first, of course, to his wife, but he thought that their baby Barbara, with her fair curls, was too young to understand. That was wonderful for me, because it meant that I had the other ticket.

They stayed the night before the ceremony with me, and in the morning we drove to Buckingham Palace. " Ginger " was keen to pilot my car, but his wife said No, she did not mind what he did in the air, but she was firm about what he did on the ground.

When we reached the Palace we were allowed to park in the inside courtyard, next to an air-raid casualty car, with its stretchers on the roof, from St. Pancras. I looked at it and thought : If you wanted a final sign of the times we live in, there it was. An ambulance car in the courtyard of Buckingham Palace.

" Ginger " left us when we reached the main entrance,

and we followed the throng up the red-carpeted stairs to the long Picture Gallery and its rows and rows of little gold chairs set facing the centre dais, with its two fluted columns on either side and its plain, dark doors behind the dais on which the King would stand.

You could not help comparing the atmosphere with what an Investiture would be like in Germany. The simple dignity of this setting : no garishness or vulgar arc lamps or blowing of trumpets ; instead the atmosphere was almost as though you were in a church, a feeling of dedication . . . yes, even though a Guards' band was very softly playing familiar tunes like the " Count of Luxemburg Waltz."

Every now and again one of the participants, relieved of his hat and gas mask, walked past the waiting throng and grinned at his little lot and then disappeared again to be marshalled and formed up according to his decoration. We ourselves were supposed to be in our seats at a quarter-past ten, but I noticed that some of the spectators were still arriving twenty minutes after that. The guest on my left smiled and said : Whatever time you held it, you'd never get my sex to be punctual.

I noticed something else about her sex. Not one of the King's guests during the long wait took out her vanity case and powdered her nose or fidgeted with her hair. They were too rapt. Even three little boys, who had been placed by the ushers on a centuries-old chest at one side, were as still, with their bare knees and their legs dangling, as the marble statues standing in niches and the portraits on the walls of royal soldiers in scarlet uniforms.

The only touch of scarlet that day was at the throats of some of the Civil Defence workers who were to be decorated for their gallantry. Most of the women themselves, I noticed, wore black, " Ginger's " wife among them, and the wife on the other side of me, too, although on her black bag was a butterfly picked out in brilliants. As we waited, I kept on looking down at that and thinking of the contrast with her husband's machine, for she told me that he was the pilot of a Beaufort who had taken part in a daylight raid

over Brest and bombed the two German battleships that are
familiarly known in the R.A.F. as " Salmon and Gluck-
stein."

His name is John Beckett, and by one of those coincidences which are such a commonplace of war, I discovered
from his wife that a year ago I had visited this Station when
he was just passing out from his training, a visit which,
incidentally, is described earlier in this book. " Do you
remember," she went on, " how you wrote that when they
sew their first wings on their tunic, they always leave a space
for the D.F.M. ? My husband told me to do that, jokingly,
of course, when I sewed his wings on for him. And now . . ."

And now a year later, I thought, he is going to receive
the D.F.M. from the King. They had celebrated the event
by having a party the night before at " Lady Behave."
" We're going to that this afternoon," exclaimed " Ginger's "
wife, and the two new friends were smiling at that second
coincidence, when suddenly there was a hush, and the
band broke into the National Anthem as through the dark
doors thrown open came the King, dressed in Naval uniform,
and with a minimum of pomp and ceremony the long line
went slowly towards him to receive their honours.

First the Senior Service, headed by a boy on crutches
who was receiving the Albert Medal. Each name was
read out and the name of the ship, but not their deeds of
valour. Sometimes a name struck a chord in my own
memory. H.M.S. *Aubretia*, for instance, because I knew
that that was a corvette, as all the corvettes are called
after flowers. So immediately I thought of the corvette in
which I had sailed, H.M.S. *Arabis*, and of Tanky, the ship's
butcher, who, when the ship was standing up on end far out
there in the Atlantic, used to talk to me about his missus
who had been blitzed out of two London homes and could
still take it. " *He*'ll never beat the ladies, will he ? " Tanky
always finished up.

Well, the Palace, too, has come through that ordeal.
I looked round again at the ladies there, all united in pride
and gratitude. Suddenly " Ginger's " wife nudged me,

whispering : " I bet ' Ginger ' is more nervous now than on any of his trips. . . ." He was just going up to the dais, the first of his Air Force comrades, and the anonymous voice was reading out : Flight-Sergeant Hugh Bailey. The light from the hanging lamp over the dais lit up his fiery hair, and suddenly the whole scene faded and I was back again over Stavanger. . . .

It was a brilliant autumn day like the morning of the Investiture. So diamond-clear as we came in over Stavanger that the mountains and the blue fiords beneath us stood out in startling relief. One moment I was admiring the beauty of the scenery and munching my sandwiches, sharing a flask with " Ginger," and the next second we were in battle. " Ginger " went into a violent spiral climb— a little bit of weaving he called it later in the mess—and the radio operator came past me down the fuselage to open up the belly gun.

As " Ginger " threw his machine about like a fighter—it's wonderful what these Hudsons stand up to, he volunteered afterwards —the boy's legs were thrown up over his head like the Young Man on the Flying Trapeze, but he still hung on and gave as good as we were getting. You could not hear their guns, only ours. When the attack was over at last and we all came up for breath, " Ginger," from his cockpit, looked back over his shoulder and gave us the familiar R.A.F. gesture of " thumbs up." His red hair was standing right on end like a cockatoo.

But now his hair was neatly brushed down, instead of his flying clothes he was wearing a brand new uniform, the King was shaking his hand and wishing him luck. " Ginger's " wife wanted to know, of course, exactly what the King had said. But what bowled " Ginger " over most of all was that after he had bowed to His Majesty, the King gave a kind of little bow back to him.

Yes, the King bowed like that to them all. " Ginger," of course, dropped the subject then, because I suppose he was shy that I might explain that it would be out of a kind of respect for their valour, for the reason which had brought them all there.

And still the long line moved on, and then suddenly it was over. We had been there two hours, and it was like two minutes. Once again the band was playing "God Save The King" and that slight, youthful figure in the blue uniform had slipped back into the private part of his house, with no parting fanfare, none of the bogus build-up that Hitler would have had as his exit. There was no need.

United, we all came streaming out into the courtyard again. There was a moment of respite, a feeling of holiday in the air, before every one went back to their action stations again. "Ginger" joined us by the car, and the moment we had driven out of the gates the first words he said were : "Can I drive now ? " "Ginger's" wife and I looked at each other and she said : "Yes, if you'll let us see the medal."

So there it lay in her hand, heavy and shining, with his name inscribed upon the rim, and the ribbon matching the mauve strip on his tunic below his wings. I was remembering how in my pocket-book there was another pair of wings. Faded from the rain and wind of a hundred operational trips, "Ginger's" first pair of wings, which he had given me after our trip as a mascot for future occasions, and written on the back, "Happy landings. Ginger Bailey."

And I was remembering, too, how when we limped home in the dusk with sufficient petrol only for ten minutes' more flying (afterwards the C.O. said : You were pretty lucky because you had the best sergeant-pilot on the Station), there had been a moment of communion strangely like the atmosphere in that beautiful picture gallery with the gold upon the ceiling.

But this time the gallery was the fuselage of our Hudson. As we landed into stillness and safety and all the vibration ceased, the rear gunner unstrapped himself and came forward, blowing on his bitterly cold hands. And the radio operator started grinning again and once more looked his age, nineteen ; while "Ginger" stretched his back and yawned. Then we all shook hands because we knew that we had been through something together and that hereafter we would be friends.

The next day "Ginger" explained : "I did not want to take you all that way and not show you something at the end of it. But my wife wasn't half sore with me for being late for my tea." His wife now was giving him a mock dirty look as we came down the Embankment, but a policeman gave us a really dirty look.

"I think you'd better let Godfrey take over the controls," she said, with her pretty smile. "You've had your treat already." Meekly he grinned back and changed seats. I had had my treat, too, while "Ginger's" wife has a memory that will stay with her all her life. I do hope you have enjoyed coming with us and on all the other trips which have gone to the making of this book.

And now there is nothing left to say except to wish you what "Ginger" wrote on the back of my wings: HAPPY LANDINGS. . . .

THE END

The destroyer ahead of us in the convoy announces through
Telephone : " Have dropped depth charges on firm c

the Radio
ntact."

Frontispiece

The destroyer ahead of us in the convoy announces through the Radio Telephone : "Have dropped depth charges on firm contact."

Frontispiece